The Pulse of Christ is an engaging, impactful, and valuable resource o₁
its thinking and content, it is also a light, engaging, and compelling re
neyed through individually but will have huge value if undertaken as a team. With helpful exercises to ground
the content and engage others in the discussion and application, this book will help bring individuals and
churches into greater fullness and maturity through APEST awareness and activation. I highly recommend
both Nathan and this book.

—RICH ROBINSON, DIRECTOR OF 5Q COLLECTIVE; FOUNDER AND LEADER OF CATALYSE CHANGE

Nathan has been a long-time practitioner and thinker using the APEST typology of ministry. This book is a
hard-won resource and will prove to be an invaluable resource for your church or organization.

—ALAN HIRSCH, AUTHOR OF NUMEROUS BOOKS ON MISSIONAL LEADERSHIP, ORGANIZATION, AND
SPIRITUALITY; FOUNDER OF 5Q COLLECTIVE, 100 MOVEMENTS AND FORGE INTERNATIONAL

One of the central ideas in the New Testament is found in Ephesians 4. The church becomes healthy and grows
when it is based on five ministries: apostles, prophets, evangelists, shepherds, and teachers. Nathan Brewer
takes this idea and asks the question: how can a local church put these into practice? It is this practical emphasis on the fivefold ministry that makes this book stand out. If you are engaged in some way with church,
you should read this book.

—MARLIN WATLING, FOUNDER OF MOSAIK GEMEINDE HEIDELBERG AND SPARK
EUROPE; AUTHOR OF *START: CHURCH PLANTING—FROM VISION TO REALITY*

Nathan Brewer's book is a wonderful summary with precise definitions of the gifts noted in Ephesians 4:11.
What makes the book extraordinary, however, are the practical points of application for each gift, helping disciples of Jesus and churches to grow in the experience of these gifts in a sensible way. He has given the church
a most helpful tool.

—DR. STEPHEN BECK, PROFESSOR OF PRACTICAL THEOLOGY, GIESSEN SCHOOL OF THEOLOGY;
FOUNDING PASTOR OF MOSAIK CHURCH NETWORK IN FRANKFURT REGION; AUTHOR OF *THE MOSAIK
MIRACLE: HOW GOD IS BUILDING A NEW CHURCH FOR REFUGEES, IMMIGRANTS AND NATIONALS*

The focus of this book is for Christian communities to learn and grow together through doing the exercises
and reflecting on what they have experienced. It is not intended as a commentary, although there is some ex-
egesis. Allow yourself to be challenged and stretched to go deeper into all that Christ is and has for us, so the
church can reflect Christ more fully. This book is a practical help to that end.

—DANIEL ZUCH, TEAM MISSION LEADER FOR AUSTRIA AND GERMANY

The fivefold ministry has experienced a sort of Renaissance in the last few years, which is why many books have been written about it lately. In contrast to most publications, *The Pulse of Christ* offers a very practical approach, which I consider to be its greatest strength. The basic principles and the exercises make it easy to discover, as well as practice, your gifting. In this way it truly helps believers grow and become mature disciples of Jesus.

—ULRICH KRÖMER, LEADER, AUSTRIA TRAINING CENTER; CO-PASTOR, RHEMA GEMEINDE, LINZ, AUSTRIA

Nathan Brewer served in our young adult ministry for a number of years. His passion to make disciples has touched many lives. The practicality of his book comes right out of his years of hands-on experience. In my thirty-six years of pastoring one church, I have seen the necessity of mobilizing the fivefold ministry in both a narrow and broad sense within the body of Christ. Few of us, for example, will ever function in the office of a pastor, but all of us can and must learn to care for (i.e., pastor) others within the local assembly. Encouraging people to minister in a broad sense in all five gifts is a vital part of both church and ministry life.

—ROBERT PROKOP, FOUNDER AND LEAD PASTOR OF CIG (CHRISTIAN INTERNATIONAL FELLOWSHIP), VIENNA, AUSTRIA

As someone new to the teaching of the fivefold ministry, this practical "how-to" guide allows me to begin the journey of what it means to be an apostle. Filled with helpful exercises for each gift, they are all based in prayer. Through this book, I not only found myself becoming more competent in the giftings, I found myself closer to Christ.

—BRIAN SCHWARBERG, MISSION PASTOR, CHERRY HILLS CHURCH, ILLINOIS

For those who are making disciples who make disciples, training will always be a priority. Nathan Brewer's highly practical training exercises place an emphasis on "learning by doing." These exercises will be very helpful for disciple-makers to use in groups with both emerging, as well as established, Christian leaders who are seeking to impact the world.

—DAN ALLAN, CRU NATIONAL DIRECTOR OF OPERATIONS, PACIFIC SOUTHWEST REGION, USA

Tired of sitting in the pews and being a "comfort zone" Christian while your pastor and a few leaders do all the work? Tired of being the leader and carrying the whole burden? Then this book is for you! Get out of your comfort zone and join Nathan in this practical and inspirational work that will lead you to get into the "faith zone." For twelve years, Nathan has lived out his own book—creating ministries, discipling many, and inspiring many, many more!

—DAVID IRBY, FOUNDER AND CEO, SURGE INTERNATIONAL

Nathan Brewer is passionate about the healthy advancement of the kingdom of God through making and multiplying disciples and planting simple churches. He is a gifted leader, practitioner of biblical principles, and a dedicated servant who is intentional in strengthening the church through the power of the Holy Spirit. This fivefold training manual is a creative and practical guide designed to educate and serve the body of Christ by empowering and releasing them for ministry.

—FORREST HEAD, NORTH AMERICA DIRECTOR FOR BIGLIFE MINISTRIES

Nathan is a fresh, creative voice in the dialogue of the fivefold ministry. He writes from a deep commitment to empower and equip believers to pursue and experience a thriving community of faith. The explanations are relatable and insightful, but the best contributions are the powerful application exercises that call for personal encounters with the heart of the fivefold lifestyle. This manual offers an amazing invitation to all who are curious and courageous enough to refresh God's dynamic of the church.

—BONNIE WOZNIAK, CEO AND FOUNDER OF REAL CHANGE GLOBAL COACHING CORPORATION

This book is a great resource for those who are looking for a practical training manual on the fivefold ministry. Nathan includes many detailed field exercises, which are pivotal to help readers move from theory to praxis. I appreciate that he pushes the church to awaken from its apathetic slumber to become a church that actively engages in its full measure of power. This church has seen the negative effects of functioning without the fivefold ministry, yet Nathan reminds and exhorts us that all are called to a life of ministry.

—SCOTT MACLEOD, DIRECTOR OF THE CENTER FOR MINISTRY TRAINING, LIBERTY
UNIVERSITY; FOUNDER, ECCLESIA COMMUNITIES: A SIMPLE CHURCH NETWORK

True to his shepherd's heart and apostolic anointing, Nathan Brewer pens a practicum for those who long to participate with the Holy Spirit in all of life's assignments. Experience vibrant, thought-provoking, and life-changing exercises, composed by someone who actively lives out his part in the fivefold ministry.

—TERRI LUSTIG, TEACHER, MOTHER, AUTHOR OF *THE BLUEPRINT FOR*
EXCELLENCE IN HOME EDUCATION AND *RUTH: ROAD TO REDEMPTION*

From the beginning, Nathan announces that every Jesus follower is to live a maturing, life on mission. Then throughout the book, he offers exercises that help us to get a picture of how we are specifically created with gifts to carry out that mission. For those who have questions about the various "gift-lists" in the New Testament, Nathan gives us clarity, focusing on Ephesians 4 as the core Scripture. A good resource for personal and group discipleship.

—DARYL SMITH, PROFESSOR EMERITUS-MENTORING AND LEADERSHIP,
SCHOOL OF URBAN MINISTRY, ASBURY THEOLOGICAL SEMINARY

THE
PULSE
OF
CHRIST

A Fivefold Training Manual

Revised and Expanded

THE
PULSE
OF
CHRIST

NATHAN BREWER

MOVEMENTS
PUBLISHING

First published in 2020 by 100 Movements Publishing
www.100mpublishing.com

ISBN: 978-1-7333727-3-2

Cover image: Colored powder burst © Shutterstock
Cover design by Sarah Smith Design
Typeset by Euan Monaghan

For bulk orders, please email Nathan@kyriosministries.org

Acknowledgments

To my family—thank you for your support in this project and for giving me a stable upbringing with a solid foundation in God's Word and in Christ.

To the Kyrios Ministries team: Insa, Rebecca, Danny, Michele, Lala, Sebastian, Nadine, Grant, René and Sabrina—thank you. You guys are wonderful friends and an inspiring community to be on mission with as we pursue the fullness of Christ together. Thank you for your thoughts and prayers to make this book come about.

To Betsy, Joey, and Anna—thank you for your efforts in editing and providing valuable feedback to make this training manual coherent and full of life.

To Jesus—you are fascinating and so is your church. Thank you that you will build your church and nothing will overcome it. I hope this training manual glorifies you through your body, the church.

Contents

Preface to the
Second Edition

You may already be familiar with the first edition of this book, which was published in 2016. I'm delighted this revised and expanded edition is now available. Over the last three years, I have led numerous training events, workshops, and one-on-one coaching, all focusing on the fivefold ministry of Christ. This has been a significant learning experience for me—training others is not only a benefit for the trainee but also for the trainer. Inevitably, the content becomes sharper over time as others feedback their experience and learning. I'm confident this training manual reflects this honing, and I hope it will be a blessing and benefit to you, your ministry, your church, or your organization.

In particular, a number of areas have been revised or added, including:

- Improvement of every exercise, each of which has been optimized for group dynamics.

- Many pages of new content, including a fuller gospel message, which is clearer and more accurately reflects the gospel of the kingdom.

- Brand new exercises.

- A reworking and expansion of the matrix table, created to compare and contrast the gifts in 1 Corinthians 12, Romans 12, and Ephesians 4.

- Additional key concepts and diagrams, gleaned from being trained in "5Q" and becoming a trainer on the 5Q Collective team.[1]

- A revamp of the layout into a wider workbook format, with space to write responses, key thoughts, and reflections.

---

1   www.5qcentral.com/about-5q .

- The translation and publication of the book in German by Grain Press. I'm thrilled this content and the activation exercises are now available in the heart language for individuals, churches, and organizations in Austria, Germany, and Switzerland.

Preface

The thief comes only to steal and kill and destroy.
I came that they may have life and have it abundantly.
—Jesus, John 10:10

I love this verse for several reasons. For starters, within one verse, it succinctly explains the goal of the enemy in comparison to Jesus' desire for us: the goal of the kingdom of darkness versus the goal of the kingdom of light. Second, it's inspiring because it speaks of an abundant life with no limits. Most of all, though, I love it because it became my "life verse" when I was sixteen. Although I had accepted Christ to forgive my sins and give me new life several years before, it wasn't until I was at a Christian youth camp that I decided to get baptized and go fully "all in." It was then I really came alive in my faith, and my spiritual pulse increased in rhythm and strength. While this was an authentic experience, the spiritual "high" hit reality upon returning home, and I posed the following questions to the Lord alone in my bedroom, "How does this work now? How do I practically live the Christian life?" I sensed a response in my inner spirit, "The answer is in your hands." I looked down at the Bible in my hands and committed to reading God's Word and spending time in conversational prayer with God every day to receive his direction and empowerment for my life. I then opened the Bible, and it fell to the verse from John 10:10. I immediately read it, and although I didn't fully grasp what an abundant life could look like, I declared, "Jesus, I want the abundant life you are offering." I sensed him replying to my heart again, "Follow me, and I will show you life in abundance."

I can honestly say life in abundance has been the reality of my life thus far as I've followed him: a deep sense of satisfaction and contentment in Jesus, a joyful heart, fulfilling relationships, inner peace, and a clear purpose in life, as well as the privilege of visiting thirty-four countries. Though your abundant life may look very different to mine, one thing is for sure: an abundant, overflowing life has Jesus at the center. I have experienced, am experiencing, and long to experience more of this abundant life in the future—more for the sake of others than for myself.

This verse in John 10:10 thus formed the purpose and calling I now have to lead others into the abundant life with Jesus Christ and is also my motivation for writing this book. There are many people in the world who do not have the source of life, Jesus, living inside of them, and there are also believers who are saved and know Jesus but are not living in the fullness of life that Jesus offers. I long to help both groups of people experience the pulse of Jesus pumping through their veins, invigorating their body and soul.

This book is aimed at people who are already walking through life with Jesus. Yet I realize there may be some reading who are not yet walking with him, and so I really want to encourage you, if you do not have the source of life, Jesus, living inside of you, to pause for a moment here. If you have never made a conscious decision to have the pulse of Jesus pumping through your veins, giving you spiritual life, then stop for a minute. Turn to the bonus material on page 229 at the back of the book and read more about the fascinating invitation to have "His Pulse in You—The Gospel of the King(dom)."

An essential key that unlocks the abundant life is discovering your role in the kingdom. King Jesus invites us to be his kingdom-agents; he invites us to be part of his team to redeem and restore this world. To do so, he empowers his special agents to be special gifts. These gifts are five facets of the gospel and are specifically referred to in Ephesians 4:11–13. This book will unpack these five gifts, commonly known as the "fivefold" or "APEST." Like different facets of a diamond, they are all part of the same object, yet each reveal a different and beautiful dimension:

- The facet that Jesus was sent by the Father to redeem us and then release and send us to new places to establish his kingdom, his rule, and reign is *apostolic*.

- The facet that Jesus restores our relationship to a holy, just, passionate, faithful God, even when we've been unfaithful is *prophetic*.

- The facet that Jesus rescues us from sin, Satan, and death, reconciling a lost son or daughter to their heavenly Father is *evangelistic*.

- The facet that Jesus, the Good Shepherd, laid down his life for his sheep and satisfies our soul is *shepherding*.

- The facet that Jesus is the way and the truth and shows us the way and the truth is *teaching*.

These five facets, or dimensions, of the gospel display the inextricable connection between the gospel of the kingdom and the fivefold ministry. You and I can be those facets, those dimensions.

There's a latent potential in you waiting to be unlocked. I invite you to join me in this discovery of John 10:10 life in abundance…

Part One

Checking the Pulse

Core Fivefold Concepts

Introduction

The Necessity of "How"

In the summer of 2015, I was hosting a ministry team in Vienna, Austria, that had traveled from Calgary, Canada. On one particular sightseeing day, we were approached by a ticket vendor dressed as Mozart, selling tickets for a classical concert. As we got chatting, I discovered he was from Kosovo. Over the previous four years, I had organized youth soccer tournaments in his home country, and as I shared this with him, his expression changed, visibly touched that I would pour into the youth of Kosovo. Out of gratitude, he offered me two free tickets to a concert on a date of my choice!

Despite being taken aback by his response, the Holy Spirit helped me to recognize the moment and the opportunity it presented. With the two Canadian leaders on either side of me, I shared the concept of grace with the Kosovar—a free gift of Christ, just like the tickets he had given me. He was once again touched, this time in a spiritual sense, and promised he would deeply consider accepting the grace that Jesus offers in the form of forgiveness and eternal life. We parted ways that day, but this encounter with the Kosovar Mozart ticket vendor led me to an interesting revelation shortly after.

I was skeptical I'd be able to redeem the tickets, but just under two weeks later, I found myself in line at the famous seventeenth-century Schönbrunn Palace concert hall, where two €69 "Category A" tickets were waiting for my wife and me! In wide-eyed wonder, we took in the grandeur of our surroundings—the crystal chandeliers hanging overhead, the walls and ceiling finely decorated with white and gold stucco, and the intricately painted ceiling frescoes. A sixteen-member orchestra masterfully played pieces from Mozart and Strauss, accompanied by opera singers and ballet.

My eyes zoomed in on the particularly talented top violinist, and the Lord began to speak to me in my heart: "This is how many churches currently operate." I meditated a little on what God was trying to show me and began to see the parallels between the church and the violinist. The professional top player (in our churches, this might be the pastor, for example) beautifully plays the instrument while the audience sits passively in their seats and thinks, "Wow, that's awesome; I'm so inspired" or maybe even, "I could never do that."

Imagine the violinist handing you the instrument to play. "Whoa," you exclaim in a moment of shock. "I don't know where my fingers go on this violin, and I don't even know how to read music. And I definitely don't know how to play in an orchestra with the other instruments."

What's needed is for the top player to come alongside and show you *how* to play, that is, *how* to live the Christian life. That's the essence of discipleship: a coming-alongside to show the practical *hows* of the Christian life: how to pray; how to share your faith; how to study the Bible; how to give an encouraging word; how to pray for healing; how to think apostolically. These hows—and more—will be the focus areas of this training manual.

Our contemporary culture is overloaded with information. As a result, we no longer internalize the data flow that is dumped on us daily; we simply remember where to access it, whether on the cloud, a website, or an email. Unfortunately, this trend has crept into our spirituality and our understanding and practice of discipleship. We think the more information we can accumulate for ourselves or impart to someone else, the better. We tend to believe that somehow this information will transform individuals and communities. Yet Paul was clear in 1 Corinthians 8:1 that "'knowledge' puffs up," so knowledge alone should neither be our method nor our goal. Transferring information to people, in the hope that it will change their lives is like providing all the necessary information for what it takes to win the Tour de France, and then expecting someone to be able to hop on a bike and become a world-class cyclist. That would be really cool, but it's not realistic! Or, in a team context, it's like giving someone all the details of what it takes to be a world-class soccer player, and then expecting them to excel individually *and* interact well with the flow of ten other teammates on the field—not to mention succeed against an opponent. No chance!

Similarly, information alone cannot be the extent of our discipleship. *True discipleship involves practical application.* Jesus modeled this for us—he equipped his disciples by allowing them to learn from him as they followed him, and then he gave them practical opportunities to apply what they had learned.

Discipleship via learning by doing—not passive information transfer—is at the heart of this training manual. It offers a series of equipping exercises—the "how"—in the five areas of Jesus' ministry: the apostolic, prophetic, evangelistic, shepherding, and teaching. Listed in Ephesians 4:11 as five gifts Jesus gave to us, the church, each will be unpacked in detail in the subsequent sections.

Those free concert tickets were a gift of grace, and led to an eye-opening experience and revelation. That is my hope for you, your team, your church, and organization. As you open your mind and heart to receive his grace, his pulse will pump through your veins as you become active. We need to move beyond learning new information and engage in practical application. If we are to pursue the fullness of Christ, we must explore "the how" of the fivefold ministry, and we begin that journey as we turn to chapter one.

1

The Full Representation of Christ

I'm glad you are holding this training manual in your hand. Jesus is building and transforming his church, as he promised in Matthew 16:18, and I believe he wants to use *you* to help him build it. Together we are his body, "the fullness of Him who fills everything in every way" (Ephesians 1:23 NIV), and he desires his body to be growing, strong, and mature. The exercises in this training manual will help you to grow and be strengthened in your faith, continuing upon the path of maturity we are all on. Several great books have already been written on the topic of fivefold ministry, all of which have a broader scope and go much deeper theologically than this one.[2] The focus of this training manual is helping you *practically apply* and live out the fivefold ministry. Before we go on to the practical application, it is helpful to explore in some detail what the fivefold is and why it's important.

Ephesians 4 tells us that Jesus gave *five* types of people as spiritual gifts for the equipping and building up of the church to represent him in his fullness to the world, but, as we will see in a moment, and in subsequent chapters, we are dramatically underrepresenting him.

> But grace was given to each one of us according to the measure of Christ's gift... And he gave the *apostles*, the *prophets*, the *evangelists*, the *shepherds* and *teachers*, to equip the saints for the work of ministry, for building up the body of Christ,
>
> Ephesians 4:7,11–12 (Italics mine)

Some of the five italicized terms above may be familiar to you, and some may be a little more foreign. In order to provide a common foundational understanding to work from, I offer succinct definitions here:

---

2   See page 235 for further recommended fivefold reading.

- **Apostolic** individuals are uniquely gifted by Jesus to innovatively start new ventures in new places, inspiring **expansion of the kingdom of God**.

- **Prophetic** individuals are uniquely gifted by Jesus to creatively connect to and express the Father's heart, inspiring **faithfulness to God and justice in the world**.

- **Evangelistic** individuals are uniquely gifted by Jesus to powerfully proclaim the good news of the gospel, inspiring **repentance and salvation**.

- **Shepherding** individuals are uniquely gifted by Jesus to care for the soul and create connections, inspiring **community and healing**.

- **Teaching** individuals are uniquely gifted by Jesus to give instruction in the Word of God, inspiring **clear understanding and application**.

Alan Hirsch, perhaps the most respected leader on the topic of the fivefold ministry, or "APEST," offers a helpful definition of the fivefold in his recent book *5Q*: "Fivefold ministry is the way, or mode, by which Jesus is actually present in the church, the way by which he extends his own ministry through us."[3] I also like how one local church planter and pastor in Vienna defined the fivefold: "They are five ways peoples' lives and ministries together show who Jesus is, what he does, and how he transforms others as they experience Jesus through them."[4] I humbly offer my own definition here:

> Fivefold ministry is five dimensions of Jesus' character and ministry that he gave to us, the church, to enjoy, live out, and equip others to display his fullness in this world.

In his fullness, Jesus represented all five of these roles: he is the supreme *apostle* (Hebrews 3:1), the most powerful *prophet* (Luke 24:19), the divine embodiment of the *evangelistic* good news (John 5:39), the chief *shepherd* (1 Peter 5:4), and the *teacher* with unrivalled authority (Mark 1:22). Picture a pie chart divided into five sections, each section representing 20 percent of Jesus and the summation of the full pie being 100 percent of Jesus. In today's church, only two of these sections (40 percent) are primarily used—shepherds and teachers ("shepherd" is a synonym for "pastor"). We are not fully and accurately representing Christ.

---

3   Alan Hirsch, *5Q: Reactivating the Original Intelligence and Capacity of the Body of Christ* (Georgia: 100 Movements Publishing, 2017).

4   Pastor and Church Planter Daniel Zuch, via written feedback form from my Fivefold Ministry Training Cohort, 31 July, 2018. Used by permission.

To illustrate, imagine I'm sitting across from you. Hey *(fill in your name here)*, you have many different roles in your life, although you are one person, right? For example, you are a child of God, an employee, a child to your parents, a brother/sister to your siblings, and friend to others. Five different roles. Imagine I think you're the greatest person in the world, so I start hanging around you and want to become more like you. I begin to learn what it means to be a good friend … and an amazing employee. And that's it. I do a great job of it. In fact, I become the best employee and the best friend possible. So, that's it, I've done it. I've become like you. Wait … that's ridiculous, right? I've completely ignored the roles of sibling, child of God, and child to your parents. Would you feel that is an accurate, full representation of you? Of course not. Similarly, the church is not fully representing Christ.

Consider some simple general examples of what happens when only two of the five are present and active:

- Try typing with two fingers on one hand instead of five. The typing will be slow and ineffective.
- Try playing a five-on-five basketball game with only two on your team. Would you win?
- Try ingesting only two food groups for several years. Your body will be malnourished.

Can you imagine the power of the missing 60 percent in the church—apostles, prophets and evangelists—being activated as well? Surely, embracing the other 60 percent would result in a healthier, more holistic, ever-expanding, incredibly powerful worldwide church!

Since Christ is our ultimate role model, we should desire to emulate him in all five of these aspects, both on an individual level and on a corporate church body level. On a personal level, each and every believer can develop and mature in these five areas that fully represent Christ. Through the indwelling Spirit of Jesus, we each have inherent, latent potential to do so, and God works lovingly in us to enable us "to be conformed to the image of his Son" (Romans 8:29). You might be thinking, "I don't have chance to become a shepherd," or "I'm too shy to become an evangelist," or "I feel I'm too worthless to become any of these." Take heart: you are valuable to God, and there's no need to be concerned. It is entirely up to Jesus Christ in his sovereignty to give these gifts, and in the proportion that he wills. And with the empowerment of his Spirit, it's possible for all believers to grow in all areas. Echoing Paul's words to the Philippians, "And I am sure of this, that he who began a good work in you will bring it to completion at the day of Jesus Christ" (Philippians 1:6). Furthermore, in 1 Thessalonians 5:24, "He who calls you is faithful; he will surely do it."

A UNIQUE DISPLAY: SPIRITUAL GIFTS AND THEIR UNIQUE PURPOSES

God has made you unique, a beautiful masterpiece unlike any other of the 7.7 billion people living on this earth. There has never been, nor will there ever be, another *you*. We are each given spiritual gifts, and even if you have the same gift as someone else, the complexity of each human being means your gift will be expressed differently to theirs. While "only" five gifts are focused on in this training manual, this will not produce "cloned" Christians. On the contrary! A whole combination of factors—our country of birth, the parents who raised us, our personality, talents, abilities, and our individual spiritual gift mix—all create an incredibly unique expression of that gift. The goal of all spiritual gifts is to empower you to serve others for the purpose of building up the church and to make an impact in the world, flowing out of a motivation of love. When expressed correctly, spiritual gifts will always point to Jesus and give him glory.

There are four passages in the Bible which touch on spiritual gifts: Romans 12:4–8, 1 Corinthians 12:4–31, 1 Peter 4:10–11, and Ephesians 4:11. One of the most common questions regarding this topic is, "How do the gifts in Ephesians 4 compare and contrast to the other gifts?" There are a few key factors that are unique to the gifts in Ephesians 4:11. First of all, *the source is Jesus*, whereas the gifts in Romans 12 come from the Father, and the gifts in 1 Corinthians 12 come from the Holy Spirit. Second, the gifts are actually *people*, rather than an *activity* or *manifestation*. For example, an evangelist or a shepherd is a *person*; showing mercy or a word of wisdom is an *activity* or *manifestation*. Moreover, the Ephesians gifts *result in a singular and unified effect* (rather than diverse effects): specifically, equipping the saints, which builds up the body of Christ towards the goal of unity and displaying the full measure of Christ. The comparison matrix below helps distinguish these passages.[5]

---

5   Note the list in 1 Peter 4 was not added to the table because it essentially only covers two broad areas of speaking and serving.

	Romans 12	Ephesians 4	1 Corinthians 12
Gifts – Which?	Prophesying, serving, teaching, exhorting, giving, leading, and showing mercy.	Apostles, prophets, evangelists, shepherds, teachers.	Word of wisdom, word of knowledge, faith, gifts of healing, miracles, prophecy, discernment, tongues, interpretation, administration, help.
Gifts – What?	Gifts as an **activity** (v4 Greek "**praxis**") of the Father. These gifts are therefore nouns expressed in a verb action.	Gifts as **identities** of Jesus and expressions of calling (v1 Greek "**klesis**"), **vocations**, **extensions** of the ministries of Jesus. These gifts are nouns, people.	Gifts as **manifestations** (v7 Greek "**phanerosis**") of the Spirit. These gifts are therefore nouns, expressions of the Spirit.
Source – Who?	Father God	Jesus	Holy Spirit
Timing – When?	Given at birth as we are created in God's image, yet, after salvation, used for selfless, kingdom purposes instead of selfish purposes.	Given originally as part of Jesus' ascension, so received at birth as we are created in Jesus' image (who is the image of God). They're exhibited in individuals' pre-salvation life via natural skills and abilities. Then, at salvation, those natural skills are supernaturally activated and empowered by Jesus' Spirit.	Given according to the timing and the will of the Holy Spirit e.g., baptism of the Spirit.
Purpose – Why?	To display the Father's character in this world.	To equip the saints for the work of ministry, for building up the body of Christ.	Situational— to meet the need of the ministry situation.
Effect – To What End?	Diverse effects: Others are served through an ongoing, living sacrifice, to the glory of the Father.	Unifying effect: "until we all attain to the unity of the faith and of the knowledge of the Son of God, to mature manhood, to the measure of the stature of the fullness of Christ" (v13).	Diverse effects: Displaying love by meeting the present need of the situation, to the glory of God.

In their book *The Permanent Revolution*, Alan Hirsch and Tim Catchim offer a helpful picture of how the gifts may interrelate in a person's life:

> In our view, Ephesians 4:11 is the interpretive center, or organizing principle, around which the other gifts listed in Scripture are organized. Consider this illustration from the field of construction. Let us say someone has a particular calling to build houses. That is, his vocation is to be a carpenter and builder. To accomplish this job, this person needs more than one tool: a hammer, a sledgehammer, a drill, pliers, and so on. At some point, he will need all of these to accomplish the work of building the house, but he will use them only as needed. Similarly, the gifts in Romans 12 and 1 Corinthians 12 can be viewed as a kind of tool belt. If I am a prophet, I will always be a prophet, but the context in which I function prophetically necessitates that I use the different tools on my belt: insight, prayer languages, dreams, and foresight.[6]

Certain people will need to use some of the tools more often, since their vocation/calling of the five will necessitate it. For example, a prophet (Ephesians 4) frequently needs discernment (1 Corinthians 12) and a word of wisdom or knowledge (1 Corinthians 12). A shepherd (Ephesians 4) will often need to show the Father's mercy (Romans 12). There will certainly be overlap, as a teacher (Ephesians 4) frequently needs discernment (1 Corinthians 12) as they teach (Romans 12). An apostle (Ephesians 4) will also need to teach (Romans 12) in order to lay foundational DNA truths, such as the gospel, as they pioneer new work in a new place. Makes sense, right? So it becomes this dynamic interplay between the gifts that truly results in a unique display.

A BLUEPRINT FOR MINISTRY ENVIRONMENTS

On a church body level, Ephesians 4:15 commands us, "we are to grow up in every way into him who is the head, into Christ." In *every way*. *Every way* implies we are to grow in the fullness of both his character and his competency. Jesus' competency in all five ministries gives us personal examples to follow, and, on a church level, gives us a blueprint for ministry environments to cultivate. This may seem daunting, especially if you are a ministry or church leader and you are thinking you somehow have to artificially manufacture these five, or even find gifted individuals and "import" them into your church. But the Bible gives us reassurance: the apostle Paul exhorts his protégé Timothy:

---

6   Alan Hirsch and Tim Catchim, *The Permanent Revolution: Apostolic Imagination and Practice in the 21st Century Church* (California: Wiley, 2012), 25.

> For this reason I remind you to fan into flame the gift of God, which is in you through the laying on of my hands, for God gave us a spirit not of fear but of power and love and self-control.
>
> 2 Timothy 1:6–7

The Greek *anazopureo* means either "to kindle afresh" or "to keep in full flame."[7] God has *already* given us these spiritual gifts, and Paul is intentional about reminding Timothy to fan into flame the gift God has given him. That implies the gift had already been given, but was latent and simply needed to be activated!

Similarly, Alan Hirsch, in his book *5Q*, provides encouragement regarding the latent nature of the fivefold gifts:

> The good news is that all five functions/callings are like seeds latent in the system. They are already there by virtue of the defining Word of God. This is a liberating idea—all the potential for a tree is actually already in the seed; we don't need to mess much with that. What we need to do is simply focus on the environment that will allow the seed to flourish.[8]

So our job is to "simply focus on the environment that will allow the seed to flourish." These are great words to keep in mind as we seek to create a culture in our churches for flourishing. If we imagine people being the seeds (indwelled by Jesus) already present in the soil of the environment of the church, then we need the water of the Spirit, and the sun from the Father, who causes the growth through his Spirit and his Word.

If we acknowledge that all five functions exist, identify the latent potential in our midst, and cultivate them in the church, it will result in five APEST environments. JR Woodward unpacks this in his book, *Creating a Missional Culture*:

- from the teachers, a learning environment, helping the community inhabit God's story in such a way where the community teaches one another what it means to live into God's future in an everyday kind of way;

- from the shepherds, a healing environment, helping people embody reconciliation as well as work through their past hurts and move toward a sense of wholeness in the context of community;

---

7   Vine's Expository Dictionary, *anazōpyreō*, Blue Letter Bible, https://www.blueletterbible.org/lang/lexicon/lexicon.cfm?Strongs=G329&t=ESV (accessed May 22, 2019).

8   Hirsch, *5Q*, 117.

- from the evangelists, a welcoming environment, helping the community extend the table of fellowship to all, especially those whom society has marginalized, by being witnesses of His great love;

- from the prophets, a liberating environment, helping the group pursue God, experience liberation from personal and social sins, as well as stand with the poor and oppressed in the power of the Spirit;

- from the apostles, a thriving environment, helping the community step out into new territory, living out their "sentness" in their neighborhood and networks by multiplying disciples, ministries and missional networks.[9]

Now that we have begun the journey of looking into the fullness of Christ and offered foundational definitions of fivefold ministry, we turn to our key biblical text on fivefold ministry, found in Ephesians. It will be unpacked verse by verse in the next chapter, and then in part two, the exercises will focus on activating the whole body of Christ. Through the Spirit, you will certainly grow as you engage with the exercises in this training manual. For now, delve into the text in Ephesians and discover how Paul's words, written long ago, are speaking to you today, and join Jesus in his mission to equip the body of Christ.

---

9   JR Woodward, *Creating a Missional Culture: Equipping the Church for the Sake of the World* (Illinois: InterVarsity Press, 2012), 204.

2

The Biblical Case for All Five

I therefore, a prisoner for the Lord, urge you to walk in a manner worthy of the calling to which you have been called, with all humility and gentleness, with patience, bearing with one another in love, eager to maintain the unity of the Spirit in the bond of peace. There is one body and one Spirit—just as you were called to the one hope that belongs to your call— one Lord, one faith, one baptism, one God and Father of all, who is over all and through all and in all.

But grace was given to each one of us according to the measure of Christ's gift. Therefore it says, "When he ascended on high he led a host of captives, and he gave gifts to men."

(In saying, "He ascended," what does it mean but that he had also descended into the lower regions, the earth? He who descended is the one who also ascended far above all the heavens, that he might fill all things.)

And he gave the apostles, the prophets, the evangelists, the shepherds and teachers, to equip the saints for the work of ministry, for building up the body of Christ, until we all attain to the unity of the faith and of the knowledge of the Son of God, to mature manhood, to the measure of the stature of the fullness of Christ, so that we may no longer be children, tossed to and fro by the waves and carried about by every wind of doctrine, by human cunning, by craftiness in deceitful schemes.

Rather, speaking the truth in love, we are to grow up in every way into him who is the head, into Christ, from whom the whole body, joined and held together by every joint with which it is equipped, when each part is working properly, makes the body grow so that it builds itself up in love.

Ephesians 4:1–16

Let's now look in detail at the key text that describes the five roles Christ gives to the church. Paul is in prison, and, inspired by the Holy Spirit, he composes a letter to the believers in Ephesus and the surrounding areas. The content of this letter has subsequently shaped and formed how we understand Jesus and his body, the church. In chapter three of Ephesians, Paul makes it clear that the *whole* body, the church, is to unpack the mystery of the gospel of the kingdom. In the fourth chapter of Ephesians, Paul continues to talk about this calling and emphasizes three keys required to display the fullness of Jesus: *unity*, *fivefold diversity*, and *maturity*.

1. UNITY

I therefore, a prisoner for the Lord, urge you to walk in a manner worthy of the calling to which you have been called, with all humility and gentleness, with patience, bearing with one another in love, eager to maintain the unity of the Spirit in the bond of peace. There is one body and one Spirit—just as you were called to the one hope that belongs to your call—one Lord, one faith, one baptism, one God and Father of all, who is over all and through all and in all.

Ephesians 4:1–6

Paul starts off this chapter by emphasizing the need for *unity*, as we each live out our individual callings. A calling is something that drives your life, a perspective of how you see the world, a passion, and a motivation. The Lord knows that our desire to fulfill our God-given individual calling has the potential to cause tension and disunity. Each of the fivefold giftings Paul goes on to explore in verses 7–11 has a particular bias or perspective that can cause individuals to pull in different directions. It is therefore vital that each one of us is characterized by humility, gentleness, and patience, so we are unified together as one body, even as we go about fulfilling our individual callings. Humility is the onramp for unity. Verse 3 is clear we only need to *maintain* the unity, not create it, as Jesus has already made us one through his death and resurrection.

Moving on to verse 4–6:

There is one body and one Spirit—just as you were called to the one hope that belongs to your call— one Lord, one faith, one baptism, one God and Father of all, who is over all and through all and in all.

Which word is repeated here? Whenever you see repetition in the Bible, the writer is trying to emphasize something to get your attention. The word "one" is repeated *seven* times. In the Bible "seven" is the number of perfection or completion. Paul talks about these seven "coordinates" of our faith, common elements that unify us together:

One *body*
One *Spirit*
One *hope*
One *Lord*
One *faith*
One *baptism*
One *God*

Paul was a master at relating spiritual concepts to the culture of the day. In these seven "ones," it is likely he was drawing on the contemporary beliefs in astrology, connecting the seven visible planets (Sun, Moon, Venus, Mars etc.) with these seven doctrinal "ones." Just as the new believers in Ephesus would once have looked to these seven planets as coordinates for physical guidance, as a new movement in Christ they are now given seven spiritual focal points that will unify the burgeoning movement in the midst of great diversity.[10]

2. FIVEFOLD DIVERSITY

But grace was given to each one of us according to the measure of Christ's gift. Therefore it says, "When he ascended on high he led a host of captives, and he gave gifts to men." (In saying, "He ascended," what does it mean but that he had also descended into the lower regions, the earth? He who descended is the one who also ascended far above all the heavens, that he might fill all things.) And he gave the apostles, the prophets, the evangelists, the shepherds and teachers,

Ephesians 4: 7–11

After establishing a strong basis of unity, Paul introduces *diversity* with the contrasting conjunction "but": *"But* grace was given to each one of us according to the measure of Christ's gift" (Ephesians 4:7, italics mine). We are called to *unity* not *uniformity*; our unity is therefore exhibited even within our diversity.

We have a clear indication from the text that "each one of us" receives a measure of Christ's fivefold ministry. Though people tend to assume the gifts are for the spiritually elite, the text is clear that this is not the case. In the Greek, "each one" (*hekastos*), means "each and every

---

10   Special thanks to Tim Catchim for this cultural insight, via email exchange, May 16, 2019. Used by permission.

person"[11]—no exceptions! And let's not forget Paul makes it clear in the opening line of his letter that his words were written "To the saints who are in Ephesus" (Ephesians 1:1). So Paul wasn't writing to the religious professionals or specifically to leaders, but rather to *all* believers, to each one of us. This text is for all of us—everyone gets to play!

The phrase "according to the measure of Christ's gift," indicates that, in his sovereign grace, Jesus has distributed a certain amount of gifting and a particular gift mix to each person. Indeed, the original word for "measure," *metron* in Greek, means a "determined extent, portion measured off, measure or limit."[12] Each individual receives a different measure of each gift. If each person's gift mix was displayed in a pie chart, we would all have a unique combination, according to the measure Christ, upon his ascension, sovereignly distributed in his grace.

In verses 8–10, Paul talks about Christ's ascension: "When he ascended on high, he took many captives and gave gifts to his people." There are three cultural or biblical references Paul is drawing on in these verses that his original readers would have understood:

First, he is referring to the Old Testament verse in Psalm 68:18, in which God is alluded to as conqueror. (You will find this verse from the Psalms cross-referenced in the footnotes of Ephesians 4:8 in most Bible versions.)

Second, to the ascension of Christ. As one of the key events in the life of Jesus and within the Christian faith, the connection of the Ascension to the apportioning of these gifts gives theological weight to this passage.

Third, Paul is making a cultural reference to a victor's parade. In the Roman Empire at that time, when a ruler or general defeated an enemy, they would return to their home city and invite everyone to attend the victory parade. At the parade, the victor would display the spoils of war—captives, treasure of silver, gold, etc., and then he would generously distribute much of the spoils as gifts. Unsurprisingly, such parades were extremely popular with the people! Do you see the connection in this metaphor to Christ? When he was sent on mission by his Father, he defeated the enemy, conquered sin, and triumphed over death. Then, as part of his "victory parade," as he ascended into heaven, he distributed these five gifts to his people, with the desire to fill all things with his glory.[13]

---

11 Vine's Expository Dictionary, *hekastos,* Blue Letter Bible, https://www.blueletterbible.org/lang/lexicon/lexicon.cfm?Strongs=G1538&t=ESV (accessed May 22, 2019).

12 Thayer's Greek Lexicon, *metron,* Blue Letter Bible, https://www.blueletterbible.org/lang/lexicon/lexicon.cfm?Strongs=G3358&t=ESV (accessed May 22, 2019).

13 See Hirsch, *5Q,* 66.

Take a look again at the definitions of each of these five gifts Christ the victor distributed, specifically appreciating the diversity found across the five:

- *Apostolic* individuals are uniquely gifted by Jesus to innovatively start new ventures in new places, inspiring *expansion of the kingdom of God.*

- *Prophetic* individuals are uniquely gifted by Jesus to creatively connect to and express the Father's heart, inspiring *faithfulness to God and justice in the world.*

- *Evangelistic* individuals are uniquely gifted by Jesus to powerfully proclaim the good news of the gospel, inspiring *repentance and salvation.*

- *Shepherding* individuals are uniquely gifted by Jesus to care for the soul and create connections, inspiring *community and healing.*

- *Teaching* individuals are uniquely gifted by Jesus to give instruction in the Word of God, inspiring *clear understanding and application.*

As mentioned in the previous section on unity, each of the five are diverse in their *perspective*—how they see things. Second, each are diverse in their *direction*, their natural tendency to move. Apostolic individuals are moving the church *forward* to new places; prophetic individuals are moving the church *upward*, connecting the church to the Father's heart; evangelistic individuals are moving the church *outward*, toward non-believers; shepherding individuals are *inward* focused, toward the sheep; and teaching individuals are moving the church *downward*, into the depths of God's Word. Third, they are diverse in their *impact*, for example inspiring faithfulness or inspiring clear understanding of the Word.

This diverse bundle of gifts is distributed as one united package. The grammar of the original Greek verb in the text in verse 11—"And he gave" these five—underscores that he has given them once and for all, and given them as a whole package. We can't pick and choose which ones we like or don't like; they're given as an inheritance to us, the church, to enjoy, live out, and equip others to display more of his fullness in this world.[14]

So we have been given the fivefold ministry as the body of Christ. In literal Bible translations, such as the NASB, the word "some" comes before the gifts in Ephesians 4:11: *some* as apostles, *some* as prophets, etc., once again highlighting that Jesus divinely distributes these five giftings for his purposes. Each one of us has been given grace for a particular gift: some as

---

14   See Hirsch, *5Q*, 6–7.

apostles, some as prophets, some as evangelists, some as shepherds, and some as teachers. It is these five functions that we will explore in more detail in chapters four to eight.

3. MATURITY

Despite the distinct diversity of the individual functions, they have a unified *purpose*: to equip and build up the body of Christ, and a unifying *effect*: to work together to generate maturity—"until we all attain to the unity of the faith and of the knowledge of the Son of God, to mature manhood,[15] to the measure of the stature of the fullness of Christ." Therefore, the third key to display the fullness of Jesus is *maturity*. In verses 11–16, Paul talks specifically about the positive implications of fivefold ministry, including this main aspect of generating maturity.

> And he gave the apostles, the prophets, the evangelists, the shepherds and teachers, to equip the saints for the work of ministry, for building up the body of Christ, until we all attain to the unity of the faith and of the knowledge of the Son of God, to mature manhood, to the measure of the stature of the fullness of Christ, so that we may no longer be children, tossed to and fro by the waves and carried about by every wind of doctrine, by human cunning, by craftiness in deceitful schemes. Rather, speaking the truth in love, we are to grow up in every way into him who is the head, into Christ, from whom the whole body, joined and held together by every joint with which it is equipped, when each part is working properly, makes the body grow so that it builds itself up in love.

What is the purpose of these five gifts Christ gave to the church? Let's look at what Paul says in verses 12–13:

> to equip the saints for the work of ministry, for building up the body of Christ, until we all attain to the unity of the faith and of the knowledge of the Son of God, to mature manhood, to the measure of the stature of the fullness of Christ,

God's Word states the five gifts are given to equip the saints for the work of ministry, with the purpose of:

---

15   The ESV translation uses the gender related term "manhood" here, but when considering Scripture as a whole, we see that the church is referred to as "she" and also that these gifts are for everyone, both men and women. I chose the ESV translation for its mixture of readability and biblical accuracy.

- building up the body of Christ

which results in:

- attaining unity of the faith;
- knowledge of the Son of God; and
- maturity, to the full measure of Christ.

Unity, maturity, and the fullness of Christ! Sounds fantastic right?

If these gifts are needed for unity, maturity, and fullness, then it seems plausible to reason that if these five gifts *aren't* acknowledged, present, or activated, the saints:

- will *not* be equipped for the work of ministry;
- will *not* come to unity of the faith;
- will *not* come to unity of the knowledge of the Son of God; and
- will *not* mature to the full measure of Christ.

Without these gifts, the body is disjointed, immature, ineffective, and powerless. In fact, we could even go as far as to say that it is impossible to be unified or fully mature without these five—it is impossible to fulfill our mission and purpose.

In the well-known Bible passage on mission and purpose, Jesus, with "All authority in heaven and on earth" given to him, thrusts his disciples into the world with a magnificent commission:

> "Go, therefore and make disciples of all nations, baptizing them in the name of the Father and of the Son and of the Holy Spirit, teaching them to observe all that I have commanded you. And behold, I am with you always, to the end of the age."
>
> Matthew 28: 19-20

The goal of making disciples is that those disciples would grow and become mature in Christ in all aspects (Ephesians 4:13), eventually reproducing by equipping others. And so, if we are to fulfill the Great Commission, it is paramount that we utilize the five gifts of Christ. In doing so, we are able to equip and build up the body in the way Jesus so desires.

Let's return back to Ephesians 4:12. Paul says the five gifts are given "to equip the saints for the work of ministry, for building up the body of Christ." When we zoom in on the Greek word for equipping, *katartismos*, it gives us an enlarged picture of the functions these five capacities can enact:

> [*Katartismos*] has the idea of "to put right". It was a term used in the culture of the day for setting broken bones, and for mending nets. These ministries [the five gifts] work together to produce strong, mended, fit Christians.[16]

"Setting broken bones" and "mending broken nets" implies restoration and healing, for example, a mending of the soul. So these gifts are intended to bring restoration and healing to the body of Christ. Could these five, when functioning healthily, indeed be a key to healing the brokenness of the church? It seems to indicate so! But that is not all. The word *katartismos* can equally be translated as "perfecting," "completing," "perfectly joining together," "putting in order," "strengthening," and "fulfilling."[17] So Jesus gave us these gifts for an incredible, multidimensional impact.

I encourage you to pause here and read Ephesians 4:11–13 numerous times, each time filling in a different word from the list (mend, perfect, complete, etc.) into the blank to get a feel for this multidimensional impact:

> Jesus gave the apostles, the prophets, the evangelists, the shepherds and teachers, to _____ the saints for the work of ministry, for building up the body of Christ, until we all attain to the unity of the faith and of the knowledge of the Son of God, to mature manhood, to the measure of the stature of the fullness of Christ ...
>
> Ephesians 4: 11-13

It's amazing, isn't it? Jesus has supplied his body with an innate potential to function with health, maturity, and power—the case for all five is getting stronger!

As we read on, we can see even more benefits of accepting and activating these five gifts to equip others. Verse 14 explains the gifts are necessary, "so that we may no longer be children, tossed to and fro by the waves and carried about by every wind of doctrine, by human cunning, by craftiness in deceitful schemes."

No longer being children speaks of growth and a maturation in faith:

---

16   "David Guzik's Commentary on Ephesians 4," Blue Letter Bible, https://www.blueletterbible.org/Comm/guzik_david/StudyGuide_Eph/Eph_4.cfm?a=1101015 (accessed June 13, 2016).

17   Hirsch, *5Q*, 12–13.

- A maturity that is not tossed to and fro by the waves, bringing *stability*.

- A maturity that is not carried about by every wind of doctrine, bringing *conviction*.

- A maturity that is not influenced by human cunning, by craftiness in deceitful schemes, bringing *discernment*.

These are important cause-and-effect relationships because the text evidently states that *if* these five gifts are in full equipping force, *then* the whole church body will not be adversely affected in the aforementioned areas. As we embrace and activate the five gifts, we see they help bring maturity, so we may operate in stability, and with conviction and discernment.

Closing out our text with verses 15–16:

> Rather, speaking the truth in love, we are to grow up in every way into him who is the head, into Christ, from whom the whole body, joined and held together by every joint with which it is equipped, when each part is working properly, makes the body grow so that it builds itself up in love.

At this point, in verse 15, the apostle Paul uses an adverb—"rather"—to indicate an opposing idea and to issue a challenge. Rather than remaining as immature children, "we are to grow up in every way into him who is the head, into Christ," as we speak the truth in love. It's an exhortation for us to grow up—to mature—not biologically or mentally, but spiritually, into Christ. Ben Peters explores this in his book, *Folding Five Ministries into One Powerful Team*:

> The goal is growing up in all things into Him who is the Head—Christ. This is a powerful concept. The word picture given here is that the body is under the Head, but not fully grown and thus not properly connected to the Head in many ways. Then as the five-fold ministries function in equipping, edifying, producing unity, and speaking the truth in love, the body begins to grow up in many areas of spiritual life, until little by little, a strong connection is made by the body with its Head.[18]

After panning up to focus on Christ the Head, the camera of verse 16 flows down on a picture of the body, "from whom the whole body, joined and held together by every joint with which it is equipped, when each part is working properly, makes the body grow so that it builds itself up in love." This verse lays out two prerequisites for the body to grow: i) it has to be joined and held together by every joint, and ii) each part has to be working properly. In short, *equipped and exercised.*

---

18   Ben R. Peters, *Folding Five Ministries Into One Powerful Team* (Missouri: Xulon Press, 2003).

Earlier, we noted that the word for equipping, *katartismos*, has the sense of "to put right and to put in the right order." Imagine you have a pile of 206 bones for a body lying in front of you. It's your job to put them in the right order. Along the way, you have to ask yourself, "What type of bone is it?" and "What position should the bone be in?" and "Which bones connect together to form a joint and allow the body to function correctly?" This is what is means "to equip." The bones represent people in the body of Christ. In relation to the fivefold, the equipping is necessary to help people identify what type of bone they are, what position they fit in the body, and what key connection(s) they are designed to have with others. Notice the text doesn't say, "the whole body, joined and held together by every *member* with which it is equipped." It says, "the whole body, joined and held together by every *joint* with which it is equipped" (emphasis mine).

To help us understand Paul's intention here, let's think about the purpose of joints for a moment, and how God gave this physiological analogy to help us better understand how to be a healthy, strong, dynamic body. Joints connect bones within your body, bear weight, and enable you to move.[19] The joints are the intersections of the bones. Are you starting to see it? If bones represent people, that means the *connection* between the bones in the body—the *joints*—when working properly, makes the body grow so it builds itself up in love! While the individual identification of gift mix is an essential first step, it's the *relational connections*, the *intersection*, the gift *interaction*, and *synergy* between the people in the body of Christ that we are pursuing:

> Since the welfare of the body depends on "what every joint supplies," is it possible that these joints, these relationships, are more important than we ever considered? We have always concentrated more on the quality of the members themselves, which of course is vital. But our character is displayed in our relationships with each other, in the quality of the bonds we develop among ourselves. Jesus said His disciples would be known by their love for each other—by the depth of their relationships with each other (John 13:35)![20]

To take the analogy further for just a moment, we know not all joints are alike. There are ball-and-socket joints in your hip, or hinge joints in your elbows, for example, but all joints serve the purpose of *mobility* and *stability*. Likewise, the functions of the fivefold provide mobility and stability. Generally speaking, apostles and prophets are pioneering and *mobile*, advancing the kingdom of God to new places, whereas evangelists, shepherds, and teachers stay longer in one place and mature the existing work, with the shepherds and teachers especially providing

---

19   "What are joints?" https://www.sharecare.com/health/functions-joints/joints-bone-muscles (accessed May 1, 2019).

20   "By What Every Joint Supplies" by Staff, https://www.cgg.org/index.cfm/fuseaction/Library.sr/CT/RA/k/622/By-What-Every-Joint-Supplies.htm (accessed May 7, 2019).

stability in relationships and in God's Word. (Evangelists are, of course, also mobile as they go out to share the gospel. However, they tend to bring people back to an established work, rather than starting a new one). In *Primal Fire*, these two groups are creatively classified as the "Start and Go" team (apostles and prophets), and the "Stay and Grow" team (evangelists, shepherds, and teachers).[21] One "team" is not better than the other; both are needed for healthy kingdom growth.

Lastly, we now turn to explore what it means for each part to be "working properly."

> Christ, from whom the whole body, joined and held together by every joint with which it is equipped, when each part is working properly, makes the body grow so that it builds itself up in love.
>
> Ephesians 4:16

We don't just want a stagnant body that is put together correctly yet not moving. Each part needs to be exercised in order to mature in strength and size. Jesus wants a body that is strong and active!

In his Bible commentary on Ephesians 4:11–16, pastor David Guzik writes:

> Some people think of the church as a pyramid, with the pastor at the top. Others think of the church as a bus driven by the pastor, who takes his passive passengers where they should go. But God wants us to see the church as a body, where every part does its share.[22]

When the body is exercised, when "every part does its share," the body builds itself up in love. By stimulating the body in the exercises in this training manual, a beautiful flow will emerge, where every part is moving and doing its share, in love.

A case for activating all five gifts has now been made, both from the Word of God, as well as through visual analogies. I hope the necessity of these five areas for the future of the church is now clear. The consequences of not equipping and exercising the body would be tragic: a limp, debilitated, and deteriorating vessel. The outcomes of nurturing the five gifts are far-reaching: more unity, more maturity, more health, more safeguarding from deception, more strength, more stability, more mobility, more growth, more reproduction, and ultimately, more revelation of Jesus!

---

21 Neil Cole with Paul Kaak, Phil Helfer, Dezi Baker and Ed Waken, *Primal Fire: Reigniting the Church with the Five Gifts of Jesus* (Illinois: Tyndale Momentum, 2014).

22 "David Guzik's Commentary on Ephesians 4," Blue Letter Bible, https://www.blueletterbible.org/Comm/guzik_david/StudyGuide_Eph/Eph_4.cfm?a=1101015 (accessed June 13, 2016).

3

Developing
Five Dimensions

In this chapter I want to look at what developing the five dimensions could do for you personally, for your leadership development, and for your team development. Along the way, you will see why it's important to cultivate *all five* as we examine:

1. The role **model** of development: Jesus
2. The **process** of development: base and phase (Holy Spirit guidance)
3. The **fuel** for development: empowerment (Holy Spirit power)
4. The **interplay** of development: full perspective (Holy Spirit clarity)
5. The **synergy** of development: maximum impact

Developing five dimensions will lead to a healthy, nourished, effective body that will have maximum impact in this world. In *Primal Fire*, Neil Cole underlines this by declaring, "He [Jesus] is best seen in the world when His Body manifests all five gifts working in harmony."

1. THE ROLE **MODEL** OF DEVELOPMENT: JESUS

The primary reason to embrace and cultivate all five gifts is because **they help us become more like Jesus**. This is the essence of our faith and the heart of discipleship. We are to follow our master to become more like him, both in who is he is and what he does. As I mentioned briefly in chapter one, in specific scriptures Jesus can be seen embodying all five, living each one out perfectly and giving us an example to follow. (We will unpack how Jesus did this as we look at each individual gift in part two.) He was an incredible role model and leader. Since we desire to follow Jesus, and be conformed into his image, understanding and functioning in these five areas will bear fruit in our individual lives and help us display more of him.

2. THE **PROCESS** OF DEVELOPMENT: BASE AND PHASE (HOLY SPIRIT GUIDANCE)

Traditional leadership wisdom advises an individual to focus on their strengths and delegate their weaknesses. While this is true to some extent, **growing personally, as well as equipping others to function in all five areas, cultivates holistic maturity**. After all, how can individuals or the whole body, become more like Jesus without maturing in all five? We don't want to just maximize our strengths and ignore our weaknesses; rather, we want to grow holistically into the likeness of Jesus, and therefore mature as a disciple, a leader, and as a church. The Holy Spirit is our guide in this. He will lead us into different phases, where he highlights one particular area of our life and enables one aspect of the fivefold to grow within us. For example, when we have been tasked with leading a Bible study, we may grow in the teaching gift, as we stretch our own understanding of the Word of God and help others to do the same. Eventually, we gravitate back to our "base" ministry, the primary, most natural gifting. Then the Holy Spirit guides us into another phase. Then another. Then another. Over the maturity of our life as a believer, he works in us, and through us, to mature us. This is depicted in the following Base and Phase diagram.[23]

Take a few minutes to fill out the diagram below to get a visual for how the Holy Spirit is guiding you into holistic development in your life, filling in what you believe to be your base ministry in the biggest circle in the center, and the phases you have already entered into in the smaller four circles. Add some simple phrases of corresponding life experiences in the connected boxes.[24]

---

23   Originally developed by 3DM. Used by permission. Taken from Alan Hirsch and Jessie Cruickshank, *Activating 5Q: A User's Guide* (Georgia: 100 Movements Publishing, 2018).

24   After filling in the base and phase diagram, to get increased awareness and insight into a clearer picture of your personal APEST profile, you may want to take the APEST Personal Vocational Assessment or the more comprehensive APEST 360 Vocational Assessment (which includes the Personal Vocational Assessment as well, and goes further by inviting up to ten colleagues around you to take the test in relation to you). These are statistically verified tests that can help confirm or correct, giving clarity to your profile. Having this information at the beginning will help you have a starting point and frame of reference as we move forward in this training manual. Available at https://5qcentral.com/tests/ .

YOUR GROWTH EXPERIENCE

Phase

Phase

_____

BASE MINISTRY

Phase

Phase

YOUR GROWTH EXPERIENCE

- 45 percent of pastors say they've experienced depression or burnout to the extent they needed a leave of absence from ministry.[28]

- 80 percent of pastors believe that pastoral ministry negatively affects their families.[29]

- 40 percent of pastors will not be in ministry in ten years.

- 1,800 pastors leave the ministry every month.[30]

Christ never intended that one person should bear the weight of the whole church and build up the body alone. The church of Jesus Christ was designed to function with all five gifts. And whether a church or company, the interplay of all five types of people will form well-balanced, healthy teams.

5. THE **SYNERGY** OF DEVELOPMENT: MAXIMUM IMPACT

Lastly, on the level of the whole church body or organization, **cultivating all five leads to a healthy, holistic, powerful, maximum-impact church or organization**. Synergy means one plus one equals three, or in other words, the sum of the whole working together is greater than the sum of the individual parts. As laid out in in Ephesians 4, the aim is for the whole body to work together in synergy: "when each part is working properly, [it] makes the body grow so that it builds itself up in love" (v16). So we need to have all five functions working in order to be healthy, strong, growing, and maturing as a church body. The metaphor of the church as a body is so powerful. Our physical body has eleven systems, each one of them performing functions that are essential for health and growth, and each one *interdependent on the others*. When one system goes down, the body becomes sick, or dysfunctional. Alan Hirsch unpacks this metaphor in his book *5Q*:

---

28 Frank Viola and George Barna, *Pagan Christianity* (Illinois: Tyndale Momentum, 2008),138; Compilation of surveys from Focus on the Family Pastors Gatherings.

29 H. B. London and Neil B. Wiseman, *Pastors at Risk* (Illinois: Victor Books, 1993); "What Pastors Face Today," accessed August 19, 2016.

30 Diane Lake, "Do You Know Why Fivefold Ministry is Essential?" Generals International, (last modified October 12, 2015) https://www.generals.org/articles/single/do-you-know-why-fivefold-ministry-is-essential/ ; www.ministryinstitute.org ; Articles: Tragedy Statistics, (Compiled from Barna Research and various other research organizations in the U.S.).

Without the fivefold fully active and present in the life of the church, we not only diminish our understanding of the faith, but we introduce significant dysfunction into the system ... Because they operate within a system, each individual APEST function enriches, counterbalances, and "corrects" the particular bias of each of the others. In fact, each function actually needs the other to be itself. For instance, your body's cardiovascular system needs the nervous system to even exist. The same is true for the Body of Christ. There is spiritual ambience and dynamic balance when all five APEST systems are operating at peak—this is what Paul called no less than the fullness of Christ.[31]

The fullness of Christ—that is what we are pursuing! Cultivating all five will move us toward his fullness which will result in maximum kingdom impact in this world. I continue the concept of synergy in the last chapter of the book. Now it's time to get ready for activation, so turn with me to receive some key instructions and align your expectations for the journey ahead.

---

31   Hirsch, *5Q*, 10.

Part Two

Activating the Pulse

Practical Fivefold Exercises
for Spiritual Growth

Before You Start the Exercises

The order presented in the following exercises is suggested but not mandatory. In most gift sections, the exercises are written intentionally sequential and should be done in progression, as they build on one another. There is no separate leader's guide, since the process is self-explanatory. Each exercise gives clear objectives, step-by-step directions, and provides a framework of suggested time, supplies required, group setup instructions, and any group leader preparation necessary. Participation can happen one-on-one, within a small group, or as a larger church body. You don't have to be ordained or work in a church building to do the exercises. If you have accepted Christ, you have the hope of glory inside you: the DNA of Jesus, the Holy Spirit. Read that again! He works in cooperation with your will to increasingly transform you into the likeness of Jesus, in word, deed, and character. Don't feel like you reflect Christ much? That can all change if you allow him.

Before we dive into the exercises, here are a few simple points to align your expectations for what's ahead. The following exercises:

- are more practical than theological;
- assume a basic understanding of discipleship 101 and spiritual gifts 101;
- can be used by anyone to equip individuals, youth groups, adult small groups, missions teams, ministry schools, organizations, or whole churches;
- assume all spiritual gifts are still available today;
- are designed to be simple, reproducible, and cross-cultural; and

- are not a formula; the Holy Spirit has to be actively involved and trust placed in Jesus for efficacy and fruit.

It's also worth noting that the exercises are not comprehensive. There are certainly many more that could be included, but the exercises in the following chapters will be a great kick-start for practicing and activating all five gifts. As the aim is to pursue fivefold maturity, it's important to do the exercises for each of the fivefold, not just the one you have identified as your base (strongest) gifting.

For those who love to read, it can be tempting to just read through this as "the next book on the list," never actually doing the exercises. This defeats the intended purpose of this manual. I strongly encourage you to courageously engage with all the exercises—together with at least one other person—and allow God to mature you and your community through them.

With any handbook, training manual, or curriculum, it can also be tempting to simply rush through the lessons and exercises or see it as a checklist to accomplish. This checklist mentality quickly leads us down a path of performance-based theology. The Bible is clear in Ephesians 2:8–9, "For by grace you have been saved through faith. And this is not your own doing; it is the gift of God, not a result of works, so that no one may boast." That grace empowers us to will (desire) and to work (take action) according to his good pleasure.[32] The same grace that saved us is also the grace that equips us with spiritual gifts.[33] And so these exercises should be undertaken from this foundation of grace.

Specifically to the five gifts of Jesus for the church, Ephesians 4:7–8 tells us, "But grace was given to each one of us according to the measure of Christ's gift. Therefore it says, 'When he ascended on high he led a host of captives, and he gave gifts to men and women.'"[34] It is Christ upon his ascension who has *sovereignly distributed* them in his grace. They aren't earned—one cannot earn the gift of a prophet or the gift of a pastor, or the other three—it's a gift. It is important to continually recognize that God's grace and his Spirit are working inside of us, so we don't strive, strain, and stress ourselves into performing for him or other people. Our world is performance-driven, so it's natural to think this way, but remember, Christ's kingdom is upside-down. Christ has made us righteous already, so we do not need to earn God's favor by doing

---

32 Philippians 2:13.
33 Romans 12:6 and implied in 1 Corinthians 12:11.
34 Though the ESV translation only refers to "men" in this verse, there is an accompanying footnote that says, "The Greek word *anthropoi* can refer to both men and women." https://www.blueletterbible.org/esv/eph/4/8/p0/t_conc_1101008 (accessed October 28, 2019).

exercises. The essence of 2 Corinthians 5:21 is that Christ had no sin and actually became sin for us so that through him we could become right with God. Yet moving beyond our right standing with God, "faith by itself, if it does not have works, is dead" (James 2:17). *Dead!* The active expression of our faith *is* essential, but is fueled by his power, and for the purpose of growing our faith and exhibiting Christ in society, not to gain favor with God.

So while the gifts are distributed by Jesus sovereignly and cannot be earned by effort, we can be trained to develop them. This means when we recognize we have been given a gift in grace, it is our responsibility and privilege to be a good steward and to grow that gift. Similar to developing your ability to play a certain sport or musical instrument, developing a gift takes discipline in the form of intentional practice. We may try and fail at times, but God's grace is always there to refresh and revive us. In any case, it will certainly be enjoyable because it is fulfilling to glorify God by operating in the gift he has given us and to feel his pulse pump through our veins.

Our physical pulse measures our heart rate, which is a good indication of our fitness level and health. Similarly, our spiritual pulse indicates our spiritual health and strength, in proportion to the measure of grace we allow to pump through our veins. Of course, it is possible, even as a Christian, to try to artificially stimulate our pulse through our own efforts, but it is fruitless and exhausting. Instead, we must allow Jesus in his love and grace to regulate our pulse.

With his grace as a foundation, I believe diving into the exercises in this training manual will quicken your pulse, as you step out of your comfort zone and trust Jesus in faith:

When we serve others in love, our spiritual heart is pumping, and we feel fulfilled.

When we use the gifts Jesus has given us, we come alive.

When we exercise our faith, our spiritual muscles are stimulated to growth.

When we *serve others, use the gifts* Jesus has given, and *exercise* our faith, Jesus smiles and is glorified.

And when believers do this together as church, Jesus rejoices that his body is becoming more and more alive in this world. Check your pulse, take a deep breath, and ask Jesus right now through his Spirit to increase his impulse of grace through you.

Get ready for new life to be infused into your Christianity.

Get ready for atrophying spiritual muscles to be stimulated to spiritual growth.

Get ready for the whole body to be activated.

Get ready to experience more of his abundant life.

4

The Apostolic Exercises
Pioneering, Progressing, Planting

Apostle comes from the Greek word *apostolos* meaning "sent ones." Translated into Latin, *apostolos* is *missio*, from which we derive the English words *mission* and *missionary*. The very nature of God is missional, as captured in Jesus' words in John 20:21: "As the Father has sent me, even so I am sending you."[35]

Yet the idea of mission—the apostolic—is not an exclusive profession. It's a calling to every believer: to be sent into every sphere of culture and society and impact it for Jesus, including locally, right where you are. The word *apostolos* appears eighty times in the New Testament, and the use of the term can be classified into four phases:

First and foremost, Jesus is the "Apostle Archetype," explicitly named as the Apostle of our confession in Hebrews 3:1. He was *sent* by the Father to save the world (John 3:16–17), and to know the one who is *sent*, Jesus, means to have eternal life (John 17:3). As he unrolled the scroll of Isaiah in the synagogue, he inaugurated his ministry of *sentness* as he proclaimed:

> The Spirit of the Lord is upon me, because he has anointed me to preach the gospel to the poor; he *sent* me to heal the brokenhearted, *sent* me to preach deliverance to the captives, and *sent* me to recover the sight of the blind, *sent* me to set at liberty those that are oppressed, and *sent* me to preach the acceptable year of the Lord.
>
> Luke 4:18–19 (my paraphrase, italics mine)

---

35 Although the New Apostolic Reformation or "NAR" use some similar terms, such as "fivefold ministry," "apostle," or "apostolic," I am neither affiliated with, nor endorse, this movement.

Jesus pioneered the kingdom of God, as well as *sending* the disciples out, equipping them as apostles, and showing and teaching them what it meant to live a life on mission.

Second, we see the "foundational apostles," more commonly known as "the twelve disciples." Clearly, the original twelve have a unique place in Scripture and also in the kingdom, as we read in Revelation 21:14 that their names are inscribed on the foundation of the new Jerusalem walls.

Third, there are "transitional apostles" that could be defined as those after the original twelve—for example, Paul, Barnabas, Epaphroditus, Priscilla and Aquila, Luke (the author of the Gospel of Luke) or Mark (the author of the Gospel of Mark). These apostles transitioned the people of God into the new covenant and New Testament church. In total, including Jesus and the original twelve, there are nearly twenty-five names mentioned (depending on the translation) in the New Testament Scriptures as apostles. These foundational and transitional apostles were tasked with laying the doctrinal foundation of the church, and some were tasked with writing Scripture. No other doctrinal foundation now needs to be laid, and the canon of Scripture is closed. Nevertheless, the writing of Scripture was not the only task of apostles, so although *that* aspect is no longer required, other aspects of the apostolic *are* still needed: pioneering, church planting, expanding the kingdom to new places, and strategic thinking, to name a few.

Is the Apostle Archetype Jesus the same as the original twelve? No.

Are the original twelve the same as the transitional apostles? No.

Are the transitional apostles the same as the ascension apostles? No.

Fourth, there are Ephesians 4 apostles, gifts Jesus started giving to the church after his ascension. They are therefore sometimes termed "ascension apostles."[36] The gifts are people, and this is part of the church's inheritance in Jesus. There isn't any Scripture that says this inheritance was revoked or discontinued at a certain time.

Understanding these four "phases" takes away some of the stigma attached to the apostolic and helps us understand that Jesus the Apostle, the original twelve, and the other named apostles we read about in the Bible are distinct and set apart in their own right.

With his Great Commission, Jesus commands every believer to be sent, to go and make disciples. Thus, while some individuals will have a recognizable apostolic calling on their life and will be ministering with a maturity that equips others, the entire local, as well as worldwide, church is to be apostolic.

When a church has a healthy apostolic culture, there is space and permission for big ideas.

---

36   Jonas Clark, *Advanced Apostolic Studies: Transitioning Every Believer into Apostolic Ministry* (Florida: Jonas Clark Ministries, 2008).

The church will have faith and vision for starting new ventures in new places, and therefore will be entrepreneurial, movemental, and dynamic. Furthermore, with a mature apostolic culture, individuals are encouraged and equipped to discover their calling, and they are released and sent, for example, to start new ministries and plant new churches.

On an individual level, apostles are wired for progress; they are responsible for, and primarily concerned with, driving the mission of God forward. As a result, apostolic ministries pioneer new things in new places, expanding beyond existing borders. Think of the apostle Paul planting new churches in new places, laying the gospel foundation for an *ecclesia,* the original Greek word used for the church gathering. Apostles cultivate a thriving disciple-making environment, and, as those disciples gather together, help birth a local church body. In a sense, they are strategic architects of the church, supremely concerned with the foundation, design, and structure—not of the building—but how the ministries function so as to support growth. Because they are starting a new ministry in a new place, the apostle must initially fulfill multiple roles: *evangelistically* sharing the gospel, gathering those saved into community and *shepherding* them, *prophetically* encouraging them and building them up, and *teaching* them the truths of God's Word. It becomes vital they train and equip others to fulfill these roles so as not to bear too many burdens and to activate the rest of the body.

Because an evangelist also brings the good news, the two are often mixed up or mislabeled. However, while an evangelist will go out and bring a lost person back to an *existing ecclesia,* an apostle would be inclined to start a *new ecclesia,* together with the person and their circle of friends.[37]

Apostolic people are innovative, entrepreneurial, forerunners, pioneers, catalysts, visionaries, and networkers, and are drawn to risk. On an individual level, theirs is a ministry of exhortation—strongly encouraging others in the right course of action—and on a larger level, their heart beats for expansion of the kingdom in all its fullness, as they seek to network across borders, to synergize and to cultivate unity. Wherever they go, they are an ambassador of the King, a sent one, spreading the message of the King and the culture of the kingdom of heaven.

> **Apostolic individuals** are uniquely gifted by Jesus to innovatively start new ventures in new places, inspiring **expansion of the kingdom of God.**

---

37   There is a very helpful section explaining this more in depth, including a comparison chart in Hirsch and Catchim, *The Permanent Revolution,* 63–67.

The following exercises will help everyone grow in awareness and application of apostolic ministry.

Preview of apostolic equipping exercises:

Equipping Exercise 1: Transforming Your City Through Prayer
Equipping Exercise 2: Discovering Mission
Equipping Exercise 3: Pioneering a New Ministry and Multiplying It
Equipping Exercise 4: Learning to Pray for Healing
Equipping Exercise 5: Missional Reflection—A Rhythm of Rest

Apostolic Equipping Exercises

Equipping Exercise 1: Transforming Your City Through Prayer

"Our prayers lay the track down on which God's power can come. Like a mighty locomotive, his power is irresistible, but it cannot reach us without rails."[38] This quote from Chinese underground church planter Watchmen Nee gives us insight into his apostolic strategy and the mighty power of prayer. This apostolic exercise in prayer is focused on tearing down strongholds.

Go pray with a few other believers in a high place overlooking the city and transform your city through prayer by tearing down strongholds. 2 Corinthians 10:3–5 tells us:

> For though we walk in the flesh, we are not waging war according to the flesh. For the weapons of our warfare are not of the flesh but have divine power to destroy strongholds. We destroy arguments and every lofty opinion raised against the knowledge of God, and take every thought captive to obey Christ,

The word "warfare" in this verse is the Greek word *strateia* meaning to "execute the apostolic." The Bible makes it clear there are evil or demonic strongholds over specific areas and people, for example in Daniel 10:13, where an angel explains to Daniel, "The prince of the kingdom of Persia withstood me twenty-one days, but Michael, one of the chief princes, came to help me." So the warfare referred to in 2 Corinthians above is required to break strongholds—the false mindsets of people in a particular city. Why is it so important to identify strongholds and engage in spiritual warfare prayer? If the lies prevail, people will continue to live in deception and darkness and will never see the light of the gospel. Spiritual warfare prayer breaks down those strongholds, because it is only by repentance—literally a change of mind—that people can receive the truth of the gospel, be saved, and walk in the light.

Go tear down some strongholds!

SUGGESTED TIME: 60 minutes (excluding travel time)
SUPPLIES: Something to write with
GROUP SETUP: None

---

38 Watchman Nee cited in Cheri Fuller, *The One Year Praying through the Bible: 365 Devotions* (Illinois: Tyndale, 2003), Day March 2.

GROUP LEADER PREPARATION: Scout out a high place in the city. It could be the top floor of a building or a hill that overlooks the area

OBJECTIVES:

- To tap into God's power through prayer to tear down strongholds over an area
- To grasp that prayer isn't just preparation for ministry; it *is* ministry

DIRECTIONS:

Warm-Up Stage (15 minutes):

1. If possible, scout out a high place beforehand and go up there together.
2. Spend fifteen minutes brainstorming around this question, "What are the strongholds in our city or nation?" These can be identified by answering the following questions. Write down your responses for future reference.

Who do people say Jesus is?

What lies do people believe about who God the Father is?

What is the mindset about church here?

What do people think about themselves (e.g., proud or an inferiority complex)?

If there has been war in the region sometime in history, how has the war affected peoples' mindset?

Working Stage (30 minutes):

3. Spend a few moments asking for a fresh filling of the Holy Spirit and waiting on him "until you are clothed with power from on high" (Luke 24:49).
4. You are in Christ and have authority in Christ. Spend the next thirty minutes praying. If the group is small, do this together, or if the group is larger, split into subgroups of three. While thirty minutes may sound long, the time will pass quickly!

Cool Down Stage (15 minutes):

Write down anything you sensed God saying to you during this time.

Apostolic Equipping Exercises

Equipping Exercise 2: Discovering Mission

Jesus empowers us in John 20:21: "As the Father has sent me, even so I am sending you." With that he gives us not only permission, but an exhortation and a purpose to go into all the world and make disciples. And of course—of utmost importance—he has equipped us with his Spirit! He is a Spirit of "power and love and self-control," as 2 Timothy 1:7 tells us. God has created you uniquely, with a unique personality and a unique skill set, and has placed you in a job, school, or among a particular group of people—a relational network the New Testament calls an *oikos*—in order to reach those people with his love. Thus, being sent on mission doesn't necessarily mean going to the foreign mission field; it's a call to reach out to those around you, right where you are. Due to the Greco-Roman influence in Western culture, we often tend to separate the spiritual and the secular: the spiritual activities of ministry and our "normal" nine-to-five work life. Let's shift our paradigm to Jesus' Hebrew mindset and merge the sacred and secular into one. As we do this, we'll begin ministering in the natural rhythms of everyday life and view the places we commonly frequent as places of ministry.

Remember, the term "apostle" comes from the Greek word *apostolos* meaning "sent ones," so if we desire to model our life after Jesus, that includes his apostolic lifestyle of living "sent," on mission. Where and to whom are you sent?

SUGGESTED TIME: 45 minutes
SUPPLIES: Something to write with
GROUP SETUP: None
GROUP LEADER PREPARATION: None

OBJECTIVES:

- To begin to think apostolically and create an awareness of your mission
- To discover the initial areas of where you are sent, to whom you are sent, and why you are sent
- To act on that mission

DIRECTIONS:

Warm-Up Stage (5 minutes):

1.   Pray and ask the Holy Spirit to guide and empower you in discovering your mission.

Working Stage (35 minutes):

2.   Spend a few minutes in personal reflection on the following questions, which will help discover and stimulate your "sentness." Write your responses in the space provided.

In general, what am I passionate about?

What makes my heart come alive when I think about it or do it?

What's a dream that's deep in my heart that would be impossible without God?

If time, money, and resources were unlimited, what would I do to show people Christ's love?

Where am I sent to?

Where do I work or go to school?

Where are the places I already frequent that I could be more intentional about building relationships (e.g., the place you get groceries, your coffee shop, your library, your daycare, your park, your fitness center)?

To whom am I sent (could be a department at work, a segment of society, or people group beyond your city, for example)?

Review what you've written down so far, and consider what first small step you could take to start living on mission.

3. Spend some time sharing your answers with another person or the whole group.

4. Create a reminder that you are sent: this could be a simple post-it for the bathroom mirror, or a whole sheet of paper for the inside of your front door so you see it as you leave each morning, or an alarm in your phone, etc. A sample text to write and speak out daily would be: "I am a sent one, an ambassador of the gospel. Jesus has commissioned me with his power and his authority to love [*fill in people here*] at [*fill in place here*] in word and in deed, so that they see Jesus in me and experience his love, which is the most powerful force in the world!" (Think of the potential if every Christian did this every day.)

Cool Down Stage (5 minutes):

5. Make a commitment to Christ and to another person or the whole group, to live as a "sent" person this week.

6. Close the session together by commissioning one another through prayer. Lay a hand on the person next to you, for example, and pray a commissioning over them.

7. Follow up next time you meet and share stories. Rejoice in efforts of obedience, and encourage and exhort in forgetfulness or disobedience. *Repeat this exercise often.*

Apostolic Equipping Exercises

Equipping Exercise 3: Pioneering a New Ministry and Multiplying It

Apostolic ministry pioneers new things in new places, expanding God's kingdom in creative and innovative ways. This could take many shapes and forms. In this exercise we will focus on the community you live in, and build off the previous exercise that enabled you to discover your mission. Remember the question, "Where are the places I already frequent that I could be more intentional about building relationships?" We now want to amplify that awareness to action, fleshing out the idea into physical presence.

The concept of pioneering something new and innovative is modeled on how the church expanded in New Testament times, but it is just as relevant today because a huge percentage of people will never *come* to a church service. It is therefore essential that we *go* and fill the spaces people naturally gather in.

> If we want to connect with young people and those who are not coming to church, we must go where people congregate ... plant the seeds of the Kingdom of God in the places where life happens and where culture is formed—restaurants, bars, coffee houses, parks, locker rooms, and neighborhoods.[39]

This is a missional mindset (going to people), as opposed to an attractional one (drawing someone to an event inside the church facility). Did you ever consider pioneering a new ministry in a new place, beyond the four walls of the church building? This exercise will help you do just that. In the directions below I have shared some reflections from a coffee shop ministry to give a concrete example to work from.

SUGGESTED TIME: 75 minutes initially
SUPPLIES: Flipchart or large piece of paper, post-it notes, marker pens, and writing pens
GROUP SETUP: None
GROUP LEADER PREPARATION: None

---

39   Neil Cole, *Organic Church: Growing Faith Where Life Happens* (California: Jossey-Bass, 2005), inside jacket.

OBJECTIVES:

- To mobilize believers
- To grow in boldness by taking your faith public
- To learn the skills required to start and build a ministry

DIRECTIONS:

The framework for this exercise is initially seventy-five minutes, but overall you have a timeline of three months to launch a trial run. Financially, you have a budget of $1,000 to work with (this funding can't be guaranteed, but if the idea is from God, I believe it will be funded). Use the steps below to help guide you as you partner with God to put kingdom dreams on paper and begin taking steps to make them reality!

Warm-Up Stage (5 minutes):

1. Begin with prayer, asking God's apostolic spirit to stir in you his creativity, innovation, and love.

Working Stage (55 minutes):

2. **Identify a Need**: Think of a specific need in the community. On a whiteboard or post-it notes, brainstorm ideas as a group. *What would good news be for people in our community?* It could be something physical like food, a place to sleep or clean streets; or good news could be something more internal, like rest; or interpersonal, such as a listening ear, healthy communication skills, or restored families.

   In Vienna, Austria, where most are affluent and don't have many physical needs, we noticed people were lonely. So the need was internal. What they really desired was authentic relationships. We also identified that the Bible is not commonly read in Austria, so there was a need for understanding God and his Word.

3. **Idea Creation**: *How does God want to solve this need? Where is God already working so that we can partner with him?* In general, sports, music, and food are all great cross-cultural connectors. In your idea creation, it is important to think about gospel contextualization, considering how you can make the gospel relevant to the context in which you are ministering, while also ensuring the gospel isn't compromised.

In our case, we wanted it to be relevant to the culture. As coffee is a huge part of the culture in Vienna, a local coffee shop was the best neutral location for us to meet. This provided a non-churchy atmosphere where people could still get to know Jesus through God's Word and through fellowship with the body of Christ. We wanted discussions to be relevant to people, so we focused on popular topics, such as joy, truth, or relationships. We wanted it to be biblical, so we reasoned from a biblical worldview and used verses from the Bible. And we wanted it to be relevant to the millennial generation, so we made the sessions interactive and relational.

4. **Target Group**: *What group in society does God want to reach through this?* Consider the question from the previous exercise, "To whom am I sent?" Maybe there are some overlaps among group members that will give clarity to this question, or maybe the idea you have come up with automatically gives a target group (e.g., the target group for a soccer camp is soccer players).

   Our target group for the coffee shop fellowships in general was the non-churched, and more specifically, non-churched in the millennial generation.

5. **Create a Timeline**: *If you have three months before the first trial run, what needs to happen before then?* What key actions need to happen? Draw an arrow on your flipchart or large piece of paper and put lines along the three-month arrow to indicate actions and milestones.[40]

6. **Delegate Roles**: *Who will take each of those key actions?* Who will keep a budget for the finances? Who will make key contacts via meetings, phone calls, or emails for support? Who will spread the idea to others? Who will keep an overview of the timeline and coordinate the different roles? Who will create content (if needed)?

7. **Present the Idea**: *Are we able to present the idea in three minutes or less?* If, as a group, you are part of a larger church body, pitch your God-given idea to the leadership, or if not, to a group of friends. The three-minute pitch is just a starting point to give your audience the key information. Beyond that, sim-

---

40 There are no examples from the coffee shop ministry in steps 4,5,6 because when we started the SBUX-fellowship coffee shop ministry, we didn't plan a timeline, roles, or pitch the idea to anyone—it just developed organically, by the Spirit. We never planned for it to grow and multiply internationally. However, these steps were added after the first edition of the book, recognizing they were a necessary and helpful aspect for the exercise.

ilar to the process in the popular TV show *Shark Tank*, they can give you valuable feedback and ask key questions you may have overlooked—and who knows, maybe even provide some funding!

8. **Initiate a Trial Run**: *What's our date for a first trial run?* The best way to test new ideas is to try them out! The goal is not to spend months working to develop the perfect ministry (there is none), but rather do a trial run, then adjust (step 9 below), and continue in a process of innovation. Consider the contrasting approaches of Google and Apple: Google uses many trial runs and beta tests, repeatedly receiving public feedback from users and customers, gradually improving their products and services. Apple, on the other hand, works tirelessly to design a sleek, perfect new product in secret, and then launches with big fanfare. In this exercise, innovate like Google, not Apple.[41] Initiate multiple runs, repeatedly asking the people attending for their feedback along the way.

> In the coffee shop ministry, people began to give feedback that the group was getting too big for them to share, ask personal questions, or even hear across the tables. People also said that the topics weren't contiguous and lacked progression.

Cool Down Stage (15 minutes):

9. **Incorporate Changes**: *What does the Lord want us to change in order to love people effectively, to bear more fruit?* This step should be read at this stage but obviously can only be implemented after the first trial runs. Evaluate how things went, assess the strengths and weaknesses, opportunities and threats, and incorporate changes for next time.

> To address the progression issue, we chose to start going through a book of the Bible chapter by chapter each week. To address the desire for more intimacy, we grew into two smaller groups and had two leaders prepare content.

10. **Increase and Scale (Multiply)**: *How can we create a culture now to prepare for multiplication beyond ourselves?* This step should also be read and considered at this stage but obviously can only be implemented along the way. This primarily involves i. casting vision, ii. praying for laborers for the harvest, and iii. developing new pioneer leaders:

---

41   See Alan Hirsch and Dave Ferguson, *On the Verge: A Journey into the Apostolic Future of the Church* (Michigan: Zondervan, 2011), 230.

i.   All of you who start this together are carriers of the vision. Repeatedly cast vision to everyone involved internally, as well as those you meet externally, that this ministry is about expanding through multiplication—God's desire is always to spread out and multiply.[42] This is important to establish in the culture of the ministry from the beginning, as it's hard to change or reverse culture once those early days of formation are gone.

ii. Praying for laborers is key, as it is God's Spirit who places the desire in people's hearts to pioneer a new branch of the ministry.[43] Everyone involved can be praying for this.

iii. Developing new leaders is key for sustainability and growth. Making disciples has the end goal of reproducing yourself. From the beginning, each person should keep their eyes peeled for someone who is hungry (has an internal desire), faithful (shows up regularly), available (makes time for it), and teachable (humble and willing). Be intentional along the way to include them and train them. This follows a simple four-step process of *model* (I do, you watch), *assist* (we do together), *watch* (you do, I watch and give feedback), and *leave* (you continue, I leave but stay in touch in a coaching role).

Some of the growth and multiplication in Vienna happened organically, through group mitosis as described above. Additionally, some people could no longer make the day we were meeting, so we started another group on a different day in another district of the city. Furthermore, some leaders moved away from Austria, but carried the vision in their heart and ended up pioneering a new branch in their city. Thus, the investment into these people initially worked for a natural Spirit-prompted progression into leadership. Their leadership in a new location gained access to a whole new circle of people, and therein lies the multiplication potential. Instead of bringing one person back to the original group, which would be addition of one person, they were sent out and began the process of starting a new ministry in a new sphere.

---

42   See Genesis 1:28; 9:1,7; Isaiah 11:9; Acts 1:8.
43   See Luke 10:2b.

Apostolic Equipping Exercises

Equipping Exercise 4: Learning to Pray for Healing

In this exercise, we want to grow in awareness of how to pray for healing, as well as growing in application—boldly living it out as disciples. As we are conformed more and more into Christ's likeness, we desire to emulate him, in both his character and actions. It may be surprising to learn that two-thirds of Christ's miracles recorded in the New Testament were related to healing. As we desire to imitate him in all aspects, that includes praying for healing.

The theme of healing can be traced throughout the Bible, with God revealing himself in the Old Testament as Jehovah Rapha, "the Lord that Heals," (Exodus 15:26). When God becomes flesh in Jesus Christ in the New Testament, "His fame spread throughout all Syria, and they brought him all the sick, those afflicted with various diseases and pains, those oppressed by demons, epileptics, and paralytics, and he healed them" (Matthew 4:24). It's noteworthy that Jesus didn't turn any requests away for healing; throughout his ministry, he healed *all* who came to him. He empowered his followers to heal too: "And he called to him his twelve disciples and gave them authority over unclean spirits, to cast them out, and to heal every disease and every affliction" (Matthew 10:1). The Greek word for authority here is *exousia,* meaning "ability and right to do so."[44] The essence of the word relates to the full authority given to an ambassador to act on behalf of the nation or person that commissioned them.

The Great Commission from Mark 16:15–20 extends this authority:

And he [Jesus] said to them, "Go into all the world and proclaim the gospel to the whole creation[...] And these signs will accompany those who believe [...]they will lay their hands on the sick, and they will recover." [...] And they went out and preached everywhere, while the Lord worked with them and confirmed the message by accompanying signs.

In the New Testament account of the church, we see prayer for healing also present, such as in James:

---

44   "Strongs Number G1849," Blue Letter Bible, https://www.blueletterbible.org/lang/lexicon/lexicon.cfm?t=esv&strongs=g1849 (accessed August 1, 2016).

and the prayer offered in faith will restore the one who is sick, and the Lord will raise him up, and if he has committed sins, they will be forgiven him. Therefore, confess your sins to one another, and pray for one another so that you may be healed. The effective prayer of a righteous man can accomplish much.

James 5:15–16 NASB

We are commissioned as ambassadors by King Jesus (2 Corinthians 5:20). As ambassadors of the King and of his culture in heaven, we bring heaven to a new area on earth, and with it more of the kingdom's healing and wholeness. This is exemplified in Revelation 21:4, "He will wipe away every tear from their eyes, and death shall be no more, neither shall there be mourning, nor crying, nor pain anymore, for the former things have passed away."

Whether physical healing or inner healing, it's the cross and power of Christ that brings it to pass. This exercise will address aspects of both. Inner healing is distinguished from outer, or physical healing, in that it focuses on an individual's inner emotions, mind, and will. The late John Wimber, minister and author of *Power Healing*, defines inner healing as:

> A process in which the Holy Spirit brings forgiveness of sins and emotional renewal to people suffering from damaged minds, wills, and emotions. It is a way of bringing the power of the gospel to a specific area of need.[45]

It's worth observing that Jesus never healed the same way twice in the Gospels, so we can never fall into the trap of believing there is a biblically prescribed formula for healing. Thus, the directions below could better be described as best practices or tips for physical or inner healing, not a step-by-step guide that will ensure a guaranteed solution.

He himself bore our sins in his body on the tree, that we might die to sin and live to righteousness. By his wounds you have been healed.

1 Peter 2:24

SUGGESTED TIME: 60 minutes
SUPPLIES: None
GROUP SETUP: Pairs; a quiet location and safe atmosphere
GROUP LEADER PREPARATION: None

OBJECTIVES:

- To grow in learning how to pray for healing

---

45   John Wimber and Kevin Springer, *Power Healing* (California: Harper, 2009), 80.

- To gain confidence, boldness, and faith to pray for healing
- To bring God's kingdom of wholeness and healing to your area of the world

DIRECTIONS:

If at all possible, before you come together to pray for healing in this exercise, spend time in preparation the day before in focused prayer and repentance and even some level of fasting. Since our body, spirit, and soul—composed of mind, will, and emotions—are inextricably intertwined, this cleanses the vessel and allows the living waters of God's grace and healing to flow. As the goal is to get to the root of the issue, this will help gain clarity on it, rather than just treating the symptoms.

Warm-Up Stage (15 minutes):

1. Share testimonies of healing experienced or seen personally.

2. If none, read testimonies of healing here: https://globalawakening.com/healing-testimonies .

Working Stage (35 minutes):

Tips and Best Practices:

3. **Get Filled with Faith**
   Pray, asking the Holy Spirit to fill you with boldness and faith. God uses our faith as a catalyst to work.

4. **Start in a Safe Place**
   Since praying for healing may be new or uncomfortable for some, engage with it first as partners or within your small group. In general it is best to partner up men with men and women with women. Inquire if the person has pain in their body, or a condition or disease in need of healing. If it's pain related, inquire on a scale of 1–10 how bad the pain is (10 being excruciating pain). This helps bring awareness to improvement after the prayer. Additionally, you can inquire if there are damaged emotions and/or painful memories that require inner healing.

5. **Give Glory Where Glory is Due**
   As the one doing the praying, acknowledge that apart from Christ, you can do nothing (John 15:5). Agree

that you will not take any of the credit should the person get healed. In addition, ask the individual, "If you experience a measure of healing, are you willing to give the credit and praise to Jesus and tell someone else about it?"

6. **Consider Laying on of Hands**

There are many references in the Bible to the laying on of hands in praying for the sick (for example, Mark 16:18; Luke 4:40, Acts 28:8). You may ask the person, "Is it ok with you if I put my hand on the affected area?" God can heal with or without the laying on of hands, but it does generally demonstrate care and love. However, caution must be exercised with this. For example, victims of abuse might not want to be touched at all. If someone doesn't want to be touched for any reason, this must be respected. Or, if the area needing healing is a highly sensitive area, you can put your hand on their shoulder and pray, but once again, only with permission. The person should always be treated with utmost dignity and respect. Prayer is very personal and vulnerable; therefore, always err on the side of caution.

7. **Deal with Unforgiveness**

Because there can often be a link between unforgiveness and healing, ask the person you are praying for, "Is there anyone you may need to forgive in your life right now?" You can explain to them some of the following principles regarding forgiveness:

- Forgiveness is often tough, as it goes against our natural sense of what is just and fair. When we do not forgive, however, we are held in bondage to bitterness and anger. Forgiveness does not mean you have to *forget* the past, but by forgiving you can be *free* of the past.
- The pain will finally stop by releasing the person to God, and you will experience gradual measures of increased freedom.
- God wants you to be free!
- It is our choice to be free or to continue to be chained to the past hurt.
- We shouldn't wait until we feel like forgiving; our emotions will begin to heal once we make the decision to forgive.

Then lead the person you are praying for through the following process:

- Ask them to allow God to bring to mind the person(s) they need to forgive. Then allow God to bring to the surface the emotional pain they experienced (if it stays suppressed it cannot be healed). This will be tough, but it allows the Lord to gently begin the healing process.
- Ask them to speak out the following:

> Lord, I forgive [name of the person] for [what they did that hurt me] because it made me feel [share the painful memories or feelings]. I choose not to hold this offense against [name] any longer. I thank you for setting me free from the bondage of bitterness toward them. I choose now to bless [name]. In Jesus' name, Amen!

- After forgiveness, pause for a moment and ask the Holy Spirit if there is anything else that might be hindering full physical and/or emotional healing.
- Have the person repent (literally: change their mind) for walking in agreement with whatever unbelief, fear, or trauma that has overtaken them.
- Ask them to speak out, "Father, will you forgive me for… [wait for the Holy Spirit to reveal an answer to them]." If you sense something, you can inquire about it and if accurate, the person can repeat after you.[46]

8. Speak out from Your Identity and Authority

Inside of you is a measure of authority of Christ, which is grounded in your identity, found in him. "For in Him all the fullness of Deity dwells in bodily form, and in Him you have been made complete, and He is the head over all rule and authority" (Colossians 2:9–10 NASB). Command the pain to go, or the certain body part to be restored, in Jesus' name.

> For truly, I say to you, if you have faith like a grain of mustard seed, you will say to this mountain, "Move from here to there," and it will move, and nothing will be impossible for you.
>
> Matthew 17:20

9. Evaluate

Ask the individual if they sensed anything in their body while praying. Ask them on a scale of 1–10 what level their pain is now.

10. Persevere

If there is still room for improvement, be bold enough to pray more than once, as Jesus did in Mark 8:23–25.

---

46 Neil T. Anderson, *Steps to Freedom in Christ for Young Adults* (Tennessee: Freedom in Christ Publishing, 2009), "Step 3: Bitterness vs. Forgiveness."

11. **Remind**

If they experienced a measure of healing, remind them it was Jesus' power that healed them!

12. **Confirm**

If it was a medical condition or disease they were healed of, encourage them to go to a medical professional to confirm the improvement of healing (Matthew 8:4).

13. **Frequently Asked Question**

What if they don't get healed? If not, don't worry. There is no need to apologize. It's not their fault or your fault. God is sovereign; he is the one who decides how and when to heal. Sometimes the healing is immediate and sometimes it even happens the next morning or a few days later. It's also important to keep the right perspective: the outcome of increased intimacy with the Father from praying outweighs healing, since it is eternal, compared to any measure of physical healing, which is temporary on this earth. No matter what, we can look forward in confident hope that one day we will ultimately be fully healed when we receive our new bodies in the new heavens and new earth. Until then, his desire is that we continue to pray in faith and believe for healing, which cultivates trust in him.

14. **Activate Your Commissioning**

After praying for one another in this familiar context, go! Go out for a bit and pray for someone in public. Look for someone waiting at a bus stop, in a park, or at a mall, for example. It may be someone noticeable who is on crutches, or you may just have to introduce yourself, tell them that you are a follower of Jesus and believe that he can heal people, and ask if you can pray for them or anyone in their family who is sick or in need of healing.

Cool Down Stage (10 minutes):

15. **Debrief Together**

    What did you see God do? What was your view of healing before the exercise compared to afterwards? Write your responses in the space below:

16. **Set Goals**

    Make a goal to pray for another person (in person) for healing this week, and keep yourself accountable to your partner or another group member for that. Write their name in the space below:

17. **Close in Prayer**

    Ask the Lord to open your eyes to the healing needs around you, and believe that he will bring increased opportunities to pray for others.

Apostolic Equipping Exercises

Equipping Exercise 5: Missional Reflection—A Rhythm of Rest

If mission were all action, with no reflection, we would go off the rails. We would [...] cram every living moment with mission activity [...] The reflective and meditative dimension of mission is central.[47]
—Ross Langmead

Rest. Everyone craves it. And the truth is, our bodies are built for it. God has designed our biological rhythm to rest each evening, and also to rest each week. Yet our culture and lives are so busy that rest often gets put on the back burner in the name of productivity: pushing harder, logging longer hours, and achieving more in order to get ahead. Guess what? The work never ends! If we buy into that rhythm and the lie that we are slaves to our work, it will result in damaging effects to our health and to our relationships. God desires a different rhythm: hard work, empowered by his Spirit, and then a distinct time of rest.

God established an important pattern for us from Creation in Genesis 2:2–3:

And on the seventh day God finished his work that he had done, and he rested on the seventh day from all his work that he had done. So God blessed the seventh day and made it holy, because on it God rested from all his work that he had done in creation.

He commands his chosen people through Moses to follow this pattern, "Six days you shall labor, and do all your work, but the seventh day is a Sabbath to the LORD your God. On it you shall not do any work" (Exodus 20:9–10). The New Testament apostles practiced rest, as we see in Mark 6:30–31, "The apostles returned to Jesus and told him all that they had done and taught. And he said to them, 'Come away by yourselves to a desolate place and rest a while.'" And our ultimate example, the Apostle Jesus, practiced this rhythm that we want to emulate, often withdrawing for periods of solitude, rest, and time with his Father in prayer.

The pattern of weekly rest is extended to us as "sent ones," not as a legalistic ritual to be

---

47   Ross Langmead, Ministry Society and Theology, "Theological Reflection in Ministry and Mission," (2004), 25–26, quoted in Kim Hammond and Darren Cronshaw, *Sentness* (Illinois: IVP Books, 2014), 93.

followed, but offered as a wonderful opportunity to slow down, rest, recharge, and reflect. Bible commentator David Guzik expounds on this by saying:

> Though in the New Covenant we are not bound by the Sabbath (Romans 14:5; Colossians 2:16-17), the principle is still important. Our rest in the finished work of Jesus is never to be eclipsed by our work for God. When workers for God are burnt-out, they have almost always allowed their work for God to be bigger in their minds than His work for them.[48]

Apostolic individuals generally place a very high value on productivity and are naturally wired "doers," hence the importance and relevance of this exercise. A rhythm of rest helps balance out their non-stop work and drive for forward progress. The goal is to be *unproductive* and slow down. For that reason, it will be especially challenging for those who are apostolic. The truth is, though, regular rest will enable you to be more productive in the long run, as well as bringing many other emotional, physical, and spiritual benefits, as you trust the Lord with your time. It will be a fight, a battle, to carve out time amongst all the demands of life—the non-stop texts, the project deadline, the invitation from someone, etc. The offer of rest is there, but we have to be intentional to make it happen in our lives, as the author of Hebrews 4:11 expresses, "Let us therefore strive to enter that rest."

"There is a cycle of missional action and missional reflection that is intrinsic to missional spirituality," authors Kim Hammond and Darren Cronshaw emphasize in their book *Sentness*.

> In the busyness of everyday life and mission, it's crucial for us to pause regularly for solitude so we can ponder where God is working. Attentiveness and contemplation are gifts to help us understand the world and ourselves, and to expand our idea of God.[49]

SUGGESTED TIME: 3 hours
SUPPLIES: Pen, journal, and Bible
GROUP SETUP: None
GROUP LEADER PREPARATION: None

---

48   "David Guzik's Commentaries on the Bible: Commentary on Exodus 31," StudyLightOrg, http://classic. studylight.org/com/guz/view.cgi?book=ex&chapter=031 (accessed July 29, 2016).
49   Hammond and Cronshaw, *Sentness*, 93, 103.

OBJECTIVES:

- To understand the nature of the Sabbath and the wonderful benefits flowing from it
- To take a stand against a non-stop culture of busyness
- To cultivate a rhythm of rest into each week

DIRECTIONS:

Warm-Up Stage (30 minutes):

1. The first step is making the time to rest. Find your calendar and allocate three hours.

2. Ideally, go somewhere outside the house where it's free of distractions, for example a park, forest, or lake. Turn your phone off or leave it at home. Resist the urge to check emails, texts, or social media.

3. Begin with prayer, asking our God of the Sabbath to bless your time in reflection and rest.

Resting Stage Part I (60 minutes):

4. For five minutes, inhale slowly through your nose and exhale slowly through your mouth.

5. Think back and process through the week. As you do, reflect on God's goodness, thanking him.

6. Meditate on this Scripture:

   "Come to me, all who labor and are heavy laden, and I will give you rest. Take my yoke upon you, and learn from me, for I am gentle and lowly in heart, and you will find rest for your souls. For my yoke is easy, and my burden is light."

   Matthew 11:28-30

7. Meditate on Psalm 23 or another Scripture you find peaceful.

8. Jot down your thoughts in response to this statement in the space below: "If I was able to do this rhythm of rest weekly, my life would benefit by..." Even though it would be faster to just think about the answer, the purpose is to slow down, and writing helps enable this.

9. Return home and take a nap.

Resting Stage Part II (60 minutes):

10. Continue to spend time doing what refreshes you most. For some, it may be exercising; for others, sleeping, reading, or gardening. Whatever it is, make sure it's not work-related or running around frantically. Remember, the Sabbath rest is all about de-stressing and connecting with the Father to allow him to refill you.

11. Whatever you do during your designated Sabbath time, do it all slower: walk slower, cook slower, eat slower, write slower. S-L-O-W.

Cool Down Stage (30 minutes):

Thank God of the Sabbath for this restful and refreshing time. Figure out a time next week when you will repeat this rhythm of rest, and write it in below. Try to make it a large chunk of the day in the future to really allow your brain to relax, your body to recharge, and your soul to be refilled.

My next rhythm of rest will be:

Final motivational thought: The rhythm of rest you are cultivating boosts brain power, solves problems, inspires creativity, reduces stress, improves sleep, recharges your inner motivation, and more. For a full list of research and sources, along with fun infographics, see the footnote.[50]

> **Apostolic individuals** are uniquely gifted by Jesus to innovatively start new ventures in new places, inspiring **expansion of the kingdom of God**.

---

50   "12 Reasons Your Brain Craves Vacation Time," Expedia Travel, https://travelblog.expedia.ca/12-reasons-brain-craves-vacation-time/ (accessed July 29, 2016).

5

The Prophetic Exercises
Presence, Prayer, Perspective

Though often misconstrued, misunderstood, and unfortunately at times, abused, the prophetic is biblical and can be exercised in a healthy and beautiful way ... so beautifully that the recipient and others around know it's divine. The essence of the prophetic ministry is receiving from God his love and perspective of a person, church, city, or nation, and communicating it for the purpose of encouragement, strengthening, and comfort. The original Greek "*prophetes*," literally means "one who hears and listens to God." When we look at the simplicity of 1 Corinthians 14:3, "the one who prophesies speaks to people for their upbuilding and encouragement and consolation," it helps remove much of the stigma attached to this gift and function.

Let's back up for a moment and begin at the beginning, with God himself. The roots of the prophetic are found in God's character: he is holy, just, righteous, faithful, full of love and passion, and while very personal, he is also mysterious. Psalm 33:5, for example, points out his character, "He loves righteousness and justice; the earth is full of the steadfast love of the Lord." Psalm 146:7 reveals him as a God "who executes justice for the oppressed, who gives food to the hungry. The Lord sets the prisoners free." And because of who he is, we, as his people, should reflect and exemplify his nature, as commanded in 1 Peter 1:15–16: "but as he who called you is holy, you also be holy in all your conduct, since it is written, 'You shall be holy, for I am holy.'" In a very practical sense, James 1:27 exhorts us that, "Religion that is pure and undefiled before God, the Father, is this: to visit orphans and widows in their affliction, and to keep oneself unstained from the world." These verses, and many more, point towards a prophetic Father who loves to be in covenant relationship with his people.

In the Old Testament, God gave individual prophets a message of repentance to a rebellious or corrupt nation or individual. Prophets like Jonah, Daniel, Ezekiel, and Jeremiah, to name a few, carried the burden of an uncomfortable message and were often a lone voice. In the New Testament, John the Baptist was the last of these Old Testament style prophets, pointing to someone and something greater to come, Jesus Christ, who initiated a new covenant as the first prophet in the New Testament.

Jesus perfectly modelled the prophetic ministry for us, and was recognized as a prophet by those around him. On the road to Emmaus, two of the disciples declared Jesus as "a prophet mighty in deed and word before God and all the people" (Luke 24:19). As a prophet, he spoke and acted on behalf of God. Jesus demonstrated prophetic ministry through his close connection to the Father—only doing what he saw his Father doing (John 5:19)—and regularly withdrawing to spend time in prayer with his Father, for example in Luke 6:12, "In these days he went out to the mountain to pray, and all night he continued in prayer to God." In a whirlwind of passion, he contended for righteousness and justice, a key function of the prophet, as he cleared the temple, flipping over tables and driving out money changers (John 2:13–25). He verbally rebuked the religious leaders of the day on numerous occasions, criticizing any misrepresentation of the Father's heart. And in several encounters with individuals he set a captive free, all the while calling them to a holy life. The woman caught in adultery, about to be stoned by her accusers, is one such example:

> Jesus stood up and said to her, "Woman, where are they? Has no one condemned you?" She said, "No one, Lord." And Jesus said, "Neither do I condemn you; go, and from now on sin no more."
>
> John 8:10-11

Amazing! Indeed, Jesus was the perfect prophet prototype.

The role of the prophetic voice shifted with Jesus in the new covenant, fueled by his gospel of grace and his kingdom purposes. Likewise, there was also a shift in the way the Holy Spirit worked: in the old covenant, the Holy Spirit came upon the prophets for specific tasks and periods of time in order to prophesy. They had to be 100 percent correct or they would be deemed a false prophet and potentially face death. However, in the new covenant, the Holy Spirit indwells believers, giving everyone the ability and possibility to prophesy through his prompting, and the grace to learn and grow in this gifting as part of a discerning body of believers. Although there has been a shift in the new covenant, the call to repentance remains. In Matthew's Gospel, John the Baptist preached in the wilderness, "Repent, for the kingdom of heaven is at hand" (3:2). Shortly thereafter, Jesus is baptized by John and began his own ministry with the same exact call, "From that time Jesus began to preach, saying, 'Repent, for the kingdom of heaven is at hand'"

(4:17). Hence, we see that repentance (Greek *metanoia*: "a change of mind") is a key aspect of the prophetic in the new covenant as well as the old.

Prophets were instrumental in the birth of the New Testament *ecclesia*, as Ephesians 2:19–20 tells us, "you are […] members of the household of God, built on the foundation of the apostles and prophets, Christ Jesus himself being the cornerstone." Beyond that, they were crucial in the explosive growth in Acts. Continuing into today—as Jesus has given the gift of prophets to his church—healthy prophets love connecting with God's heart and communicating his love and perspective. Far from being isolated stars, those graced with the gift of the prophetic are part of the larger body of Christ and should be part of a local church body, meaning they are to function in fellowship, accountability, and in cooperation, with the other gifts and parts of the body.

The individual's prophetic spiritual gifting is expressed in both a *vertical* dimension of focus on the Father's heart as well a *horizontal* dimension of focusing on people.

A healthy *vertical* prophetic culture in a church will generate a strong loyalty and faithfulness to God. There will be a hunger to connect with his heart in worship and prayer, and a sense of holiness, righteousness, and justice will be present. This will result in conviction of sin, and a good understanding and practice of repentance. Through prophetic culture, the body will be regularly encouraged and built up, and when specific prophetic words are given, they will be tested and discerned together. The church will be led by the Spirit with regular rhythms of seeking God's will in all areas. A mature prophetic church will express the prophetic into the world, living out God's prophetic nature in the city or local area, such as taking a stand for justice in some way.

The *horizontal* dimension of the prophetic relates to sensing the Father's heart for a specific person, group, church, or situation in society in order to put it into action to help people via avenues of social justice, such as anti-human trafficking. Prophets are guiding voices for people and for the church. Formerly referred to as "seers" in the Old Testament, today's prophetic eyes also see issues in the spiritual realm that help guide the person or church into God's alignment. They are gifted in challenging the status quo, yet because of that, can be in danger of becoming critical when they see the cracks in a system or shortcomings of a person. Because their natural tendency is to bluntly "tell it like it is," it is all the more important to first go to God with what they perceive and seek his thoughts and his heart about the person, situation, or church before verbally communicating any message. The challenge of the prophet is always to communicate that message in love. Without love, it is "nothing" (1 Corinthians 13:2).

While some specific people have been graced with a large portion of the prophetic (Ephesians 4:7,11) and will mature to the point of equipping others in the gift, it is biblical to expect all believers who are filled with the Holy Spirit to have the ability to prophesy and should desire to do so. In Paul's letter to the Corinthians, he exhorts believers to "Follow the way of love and eagerly desire gifts of the Spirit, especially prophecy" (1 Corinthians 14:1 NIV). Therefore, the gift of prophecy involves a spectrum of growth and maturity over time.

Because their inclination is to be alone with God, waiting and listening, prophets more than others need to intentionally seek out the other four of the fivefold for health and full synergy in order to "[build] up the body of Christ, until we all attain to […] the measure of the stature of the fullness of Christ" (Ephesians 4:12–13).

Prophets often tend to be gifted creatively—they may be artists, musicians, writers, designers to name but a few—and potentially live out their calling within those industries. Alternatively, they may work in the business world as a consultant, or within an organization seeking social justice.

> **Prophetic individuals** are uniquely gifted by Jesus to creatively connect to and express the Father's heart, inspiring **faithfulness to God and justice in the world**.

The following exercises will help everyone grow in awareness and application of prophecy.

Preview of prophetic equipping exercises:

Equipping Exercise 1: Receiving from God Our Father
Equipping Exercise 2: Forming a Prophetic Word for Another Person
Equipping Exercise 3: Handling Negative Impressions
Equipping Exercise 4: Taking a Stand Against Injustice
Equipping Exercise 5: Functioning Together as a Body

Prophetic Equipping Exercises

Equipping Exercise 1: Receiving From God Our Father

The essence of the prophetic ministry is receiving our heavenly Father's love and perspective of a person, church, or nation, and sharing it for the purpose of encouragement, strengthening and comfort. Sensing God's communication through his Spirit is the basis for prophecy. While there is no set formula for hearing God speak, there are certainly principles that help. Drawing from "4 Keys to Hearing God's Voice" by Mark and Patti Virkler, we will take time to relax and receive from our Father.[51] Just as we have received forgiveness, received salvation, received mercy and grace, and receive things in faith regularly, we are also able to receive something for our situation in life right now. Many Christians struggle to hear from God or say they can't hear him, but that's a lie from the enemy. John 10:27 assures us, "My sheep hear my voice, and I know them, and they follow me." Come to him with an expectation that he will speak—he loves to communicate with his children!

SUGGESTED TIME: 45 minutes
SUPPLIES: Bible, pen, paper
GROUP SETUP: None
GROUP LEADER PREPARATION: Pray; optional quiet worship or instrumental music

OBJECTIVES:

- To receive from God our Father something that strengthens, encourages, or comforts you personally
- To grow in confidence that you can hear his voice as he communicates with you uniquely

---

51   Mark and Patti Virkler, "4 Keys to Hearing God's Voice," Communion With God Ministries, www.cwgministries.org/Four-Keys-to-Hearing-Gods-Voice (accessed October 28, 2019). Their four steps are stop, look, listen, and write, which I have adapted as steps 4, 5, 6, and 7 in the exercise.

DIRECTIONS:

Warm-Up Stage (10 Minutes):

1. **Begin** by reading Hebrews 4:16, 10:22 and John 10:27.

2. **Pray** that God accomplishes the objectives above and for his presence and love to fill the room.

3. **Confess**: "If we confess our sins, he is faithful and just to forgive us our sins and to cleanse us from all unrighteousness" (1 John 1:9). Like cleaning out clogged pipes, confessing our sins removes blockages and helps the flow of communication. Spend a minute or two confessing anything to the Lord.

Working Stage (25 Minutes):

4. **Relax and Tune Out**: Prepare your heart and mind to receive from the Lord. Relax by taking a few deep breaths. Tune out things around you. If things pop into your mind (e.g., to-dos), jot a short note in the space below to clear it from your mind. Invite the Holy Spirit to come into your mind, fill your heart, and speak to you in a personal way. This process of relaxing and tuning out may take a few minutes, so just be patient and wait in his presence.

5. **Focus and Tune In**: Make sure you are relaxed, yet still alert. Don't fall asleep! With eyes closed, focus on Jesus, as if you were sitting across from him. Tune into his presence. Tell him about a situation that's worrying you right now or that you are discouraged about. Use the space below to write it down in a few phrases, directly addressing him.

6. **Sense**: A vast majority of prophecy is simply drawing directly from what the Bible already says (e.g., a Bible verse that "pops into mind"), yet it can also be more unusual or creative, in the form of a picture or a short "video clip" that plays in your mind's eye, a banner across your mind, a strong feeling, a number, a song, an object in the room or an object outside the window. God is a limitless God. He is also a personal God, so because you are unique, he communicates to you in a unique way.

7. **Write it Down**: After you sense something, write it down in the space below. Even if you are unsure if it was from God, just write it down. Often our own doubt or over-analysis prevents us from accepting something from him. The next step will deal with evaluation and testing what you have seen or heard. Writing down prophecy is exemplified several times in Scripture: Isaiah was told to, "Take a large scroll, and write on it with a man's pen" what the Lord had shown him (Isaiah 8:1 NKJV); Habakkuk was exhorted, "Write the vision; make it plain on tablets" (Habakkuk 2:1); John was commanded to "write what you see in a book" regarding the churches (Revelation 1:11); and again "write this down" regarding the vision of the New Jerusalem (Revelation 21:5). Writing helps us to evaluate and to remember what we have seen or heard, and it gives us something to refer back to in the future.

Cool Down Stage (10 Minutes):

8. **Evaluate it**: "test everything; hold fast what is good" (1 Thessalonians 5:21). Here are a few questions to use as filters to help test prophecy. Write down your evaluation in the space provided:

Is what I wrote in line with Scripture? Can you give one or two examples?

Is what I wrote in line with the Father's character? Can you give one or two examples?

Does it strengthen, encourage, or comfort? How so?

What's the spirit behind the prophecy—is it the Spirit of God, the spirit of man, or an evil spirit? (1 John 4:13)

How does it fit with my life situation? (Keep in mind it could be more relevant next week or month, etc.)

9. **Ask about it**: Ask the rest of the group any questions if unsure about something, or, if you're doing this alone as part of your quiet time, email your questions or thoughts to a trusted Christian friend. This helps with discernment.

10. **Keep it**: It is always helpful to refer back to the Lord's encouraging words when you are discouraged. Also, while it may not feel so relevant right now, it could be applicable to the future.

Do not be discouraged if you feel like you can't sense the Lord's voice. It's a gradual learning process, like a skill that can be continually improved. Similar to spending time with another person and getting to know them, spending time with the Lord in his Word, in prayer, and in abiding will deepen intimacy and, in turn, will help you more quickly and easily sense his voice.

Prophetic Equipping Exercises

Equipping Exercise 2: Forming a Prophetic Word for Another Person

Now that a basic understanding of the prophetic has been laid and exercised—receiving from God his heart and thoughts—the next step is to use this for someone else. Remember, all spiritual gifts are given by God for the benefit of others, to be exercised in love for the glory of Christ. In this prophetic equipping exercise, individuals will choose numbers at random and compose a written word of encouragement, strengthening, and/or comfort to be exchanged with someone else. The random draw helps remove biases and emphasizes trust in the Lord.

SUGGESTED TIME: 45 minutes
SUPPLIES: Paper, pens, Bibles, scissors, and two small baskets
GROUP SETUP: A set up that allows face-to-face interaction
GROUP LEADER PREPARATION: On a sheet of paper, write numbers down 1, 2, 3, 4, etc., for the number of people present, leaving space in between each so that you can cut or tear around the numbers and place them in a basket (or your cupped hands). Mix them up.

OBJECTIVES:

- To learn how to form a prophetic word for someone else
- To strengthen, encourage, and comfort someone else
- To grow in confidence in hearing God's voice

DIRECTIONS:

Warm-Up Stage (5 minutes):

1. **Pull out a number** from the basket at random. Do not show this number to anyone. The number represents a person in the room you will pray and write for. Copy the number to the top of a personal sheet of paper. When all numbers have been drawn, place them back into the basket.

2. **Prepare your heart and mind** to receive from the Lord. Relax by taking a few deep breaths. Invite the Holy Spirit to come and speak to you in a personal way. Wait in his presence.

3. **Prepare your heart and mind with repentance**: "If we confess our sins, he is faithful and just to forgive us our sins and to cleanse us from all unrighteousness" (1 John 1:9). Like cleaning out clogged pipes, this removes blockages and helps the flow of communication. Spend a minute or two confessing anything to the Lord.

Working Stage (20 minutes):

4. Begin to ask the Lord some questions to guide you ... *Father, what do you want to say to this person (number 4, for example)? What do you think about them? How do you want to strengthen them and build them up? How do you want to encourage them? How do you want to comfort them?* Obviously, other questions can be asked as well, but these are solid general ones to start with.

5. As you hear, see, or sense answers, jot them down on your piece of paper. It may be so subtle that you doubt it's even God's voice, but just step out in faith and jot them down. It might be key words, phrases, or whole sentences in the form of a letter. It could also be a sketch or drawing with a description. When you are finished, fold the piece of paper so it's confidential, *write the number on the outside,* so it can be easily identified, and place it into the second basket.

6. When everyone is finished, and all papers are in the basket, draw a number again from the first basket. This is your personal number.

7. Have someone call out the written papers in the second basket and pass them out accordingly to the person who has the matching personal number.

8. Take time to read it, think about it, and enjoy it!

Cool Down Stage (20 minutes):

9. **Evaluate it**: "... test everything; hold fast what is good" (1 Thessalonians 5:21). Here are a few filters to help you test what you received. Write down your evaluation in the space provided:

Is the content on your paper in line with Scripture? Can you give one or two examples?

Is the content in line with the Father's character? Can you give one or two examples?

Does it strengthen, encourage, or comfort? How so?

What's the spirit behind the prophecy—is it the Spirit of God, the spirit of man, or an evil spirit? (1 John 4:13)

Does it glorify Jesus? Why or why not?

Is it manipulative or controlling in any way?

How does it fit to your life situation? (Keep in mind it could be more relevant next week, or month, etc.)

10. **Ask about it**: Ask the rest of the group any questions if you are unsure about something. This helps with discernment.

11. **Keep it**: It is always helpful to refer back to the Lord's encouraging words when you are discouraged. Furthermore, it's worthwhile revisiting a prophetic word to see how much progress has been made into this word. Lastly, should it become fulfilled, it's time to give thanks and praise. Thank the Lord, thank the person who gave the word (which will encourage them that they were hearing the Lord well), and share the testimony with other believers (which gives God glory and increases the faith of others).

Prophetic Equipping Exercises

Equipping Exercise 3: Handling Negative Impressions

As you grow in the prophetic area, impressions will come more quickly and clearly as you pray for someone. But what if the impression you receive is difficult or even negative? A sign of maturity and growth is being able to communicate a prophetic word in the *right timing*, with a *positive framework* and *tone*. These three areas will be the focus of this exercise.

God often uses the prophetic to challenge the status quo and help see a new and better way that aligns with his purposes. Seeing the cracks in a system or shortcomings of a person, however, can often come across as critical or blunt, which could damage a relationship. Therefore, it's important not to speak impulsively, but rather to go to God and meditate on a word or impression for a while, or, if you are praying with a person, pause and listen in the moment as you inquire how to speak out. Communicating truth is important, of course, yet has to be combined with grace and love, in the same way Jesus operated, especially when dealing with delicate situations.

Revelation chapters 2–3 contains prophetic words to the churches in Asia that were effective words of correction in order to achieve God's purposes. Graham Cooke, in his book *Prophecy & Responsibility*, gives an excellent example from Revelation 2:2–6 of how to handle words of correction, using the familiar passage to the church in Ephesus:

> [2] I know your works, your toil and your patient endurance, and how you cannot bear with those who are evil, but have tested those who call themselves apostles and are not, and found them to be false. [3] I know you are enduring patiently and bearing up for my name's sake, and you have not grown weary. [4] But I have this against you, that you have abandoned the love you had at first. [5] Remember therefore from where you have fallen; repent, and do the works you did at first. If not, I will come to you and remove your lampstand from its place, unless you repent. [6] Yet this you have: you hate the works of the Nicolaitans, which I also hate.

- Understand the situation that the church or person is facing. (v.2)
- Give praise where it is relevant. (vv.3,6)
- Highlight the area where God desires change. (v.4)
- Give a clear call to action. (v.5)[52]

---

52   Graham Cooke, *Prophecy & Responsibility* (British Columbia: Brilliant Book House, 2010), 101.

This is a good pattern to follow. We want to see the person (or church) in the way God sees them and therefore speak to them in the way God would speak to them.

SUGGESTED TIME: 50 minutes
SUPPLIES: None
GROUP SETUP: A quiet and safe atmosphere
GROUP LEADER PREPARATION: If others do not have the training manual, make copies of this exercise as a handout for participants to be able to fill out the matrix at the end for themselves

OBJECTIVES:

- To learn how to reformulate a difficult or negative impression in prayer
- To grow in maturity in the timing, positive framework, and tone of delivering a prophetic word

DIRECTIONS:

In this exercise, you will first learn some key principles for handling negative prophetic impressions. It's important to be familiar with these principles, so you are confident to apply them if you are ever in a situation where you are praying for someone and sense something negative. Using the five key questions below as a framework will enable you to communicate with grace and truth. Read through the content in the steps below, jotting down your own reflections as you read, and then apply the principles in the matrix at the end, before finally applying them to a situation you are currently facing.

Warm-Up Stage (1 minute):

1. **Open in Prayer**: Ask the Father to help you communicate his love through grace and truth in delicate situations.

Working Stage (40 minutes):

2. **Timing**: In general, if you sense something negative about the person's life or character as you pray, it's important to *pause and silently* ask the Lord what he wants to do in their situation. To be clear, don't impulsively write or speak out the first thing you sense (the negative issue), *wait* on the Lord and speak out the second thing (the positive). Speaking out the negative thing could expose a person in front of

a group, embarrassing them and potentially damaging their character. (If you are *not* with the person you are praying for and discern something negative, use the time to chew on it and shape it carefully. Waiting forty-eight hours to share it is a good timeframe, or you may even "put it on the shelf" longer to revisit at a later date. However, don't allow that to be an excuse for not delivering the word in a timely manner.)

Key question to remember: *Should I speak this out now, or wait on you Lord?*

3. **Positive Framework**: From what you perceive in the life of the person, reframe it positively. If you sense there are sin issues that need to be addressed, do not expose the sin, but do exhort a clear call to repentance. When spoken with a base of grace, even repentance becomes positive, as it restores intimacy with the Father, as well as restoring relationships and fellowship. The goal is to allow God's loving kindness to lead them to repentance (Romans 2:4) and allow the Holy Spirit to do his job of conviction (John 16:8). To reframe things positively, pray in the opposite spirit, using words to bless, not to curse. For example, if you sense the person is filled with anxiety and fear, rather than calling that out, bless them with peace and courage. You could speak out something like this: "I sense that God wants to cooperate with you to bring *(peace and courage, for example)* into your life. I bless you with his peace and his courage."

Key question to remember: *How can I reframe this negative issue positively?*

4. **Tone**: The tone of delivery should match the content. For example, if you sense the Lord wants to relieve anxiety by leading someone to peaceful waters and restoring their soul, you wouldn't want to shout it loudly or say it in an aggressive tone; on the contrary, it would need to be spoken in a soft, gentle, peaceful tone, probably spoken out rather slowly.

Key question to remember: *What's the best tone to deliver this word?*

5. **Attribute of God**: Supplement the timing, positive framework, and tone you have with some encouragement of how God wants to reveal himself in this situation. (e.g., as their Rock, their Refuge, their Provider, their Healer, their Peace, their Loving Father, their Freedom, etc.)

   Key question to remember: *Who does God want to reveal himself as for them?*

6. **Verse**: Lastly, we want to give them an anchor from God's Word to hold on to, which reflects the positive framework and their situation.

   Key question to remember: *What Bible verse is applicable here?*

7. **Practical Examples**: Let's try it! Using the following examples of different issues in the far left column, work in pairs to fill in the chart, reformulating the negative issue into a positive framework that is encouraging, strengthening, and comforting, adding a description of the tone you would use, an attribute of God, and a Bible verse. Since timing is an issue that is only relevant in a real-life situation of prayer for someone in person, it is not included in the chart.

Issue	Positive Framework	Description of Tone	Attribute of God	Bible Verse
You sense the person is full of **fear** and **anxiety**.				
You perceive that obsessive **control** over his/her schedule and others is an issue.				
You feel the Lord saying that there are issues of **dishonesty**.				
You sense the person may be struggling with **lust** or **pornography**.				
You discern there is unhealthy **competition** going on in an area of his/her life (e.g., amongst work colleagues or siblings).				

8. **Written Formulation**: Choose one issue from the list above to write out fully in paragraph form below and ask a mature believer to give you honest feedback. Try to incorporate their suggestions next time you are praying for someone.

Cool Down Stage (10 minutes):

9. **Real-Life Situation**: Finally, think of a real-life situation of a church or person you know, and use the pattern given in the matrix to pray through it, writing down a paragraph formulation in the space below. Additionally, re-read the "Timing" point and pray specifically about when this word should be delivered.

Prophetic Equipping Exercises

Equipping Exercise 4: Taking a Stand Against Injustice

As mentioned in the overview, the prophetic spiritual gifting is expressed in both a *vertical* dimension of seeking the Father's heart as well a *horizontal* dimension of taking action on behalf of others. This horizontal relationship often expresses itself via avenues of social justice. The world was beautiful and perfect when our Father created it, but through sin it has been damaged and broken. As we partner with him, we have the privilege to restore creation and people. Psalm 97:2b tells us, "righteousness and justice are the foundation of His throne," so we are expressing the Father's heart and his kingdom when we take a stand for righteousness and justice in this world.

While the previous exercises have focused on the vertical dimension, this exercise will give you an opportunity to grow in prophetic awareness and application in the horizontal dimension.[53]

SUGGESTED TIME: 50 minutes
SUPPLIES: None
GROUP SETUP: None
GROUP LEADER PREPARATION: None

OBJECTIVES:

* To understand and internalize God's heart for justice
* To grow in maturity in the prophetic through *awareness* of the horizontal dimension
* To grow in maturity in the prophetic through *application* of the horizontal dimension

---

53   This exercise was co-created via a Zoom conversation with Cath Livesey on March 11, 2019. For more about her ministry, visit www.accessibleprophecy.com .

DIRECTIONS:

Warm-Up Stage (15 minutes):

1. Read these verses out loud together: Genesis 18:19, Isaiah 61:1-4, Matthew 6:33, Psalm 33:5, 82:3-4, Psalm 146:5-10, Proverbs 31:8-9, Micah 6:8, Zechariah 7:9-11, Luke 4:16-19, James 1:27, Revelation 21:3-5.
2. Spend a few minutes in prayer, asking the Father to give you his heart of justice for this world.

Working Stage (30 minutes):

3. As a group, brainstorm specific issues of injustice in the world today, and write them on various colored post-it notes. Then post them on a wall or flip chart for all to see. The issues can be anything from persecution, to poverty, human trafficking, orphans, homelessness, false imprisonment, or food waste.

4. God has given each of us a measure of "holy discontent" about these issues, and usually there is one that is very near to your heart. Narrow down the list to one specific issue you are passionate about as an individual, or choose one as a group, and write it below:

5. Come to a place of rest and listen to the Father. Ask him what he thinks and how he feels about this issue and write it down.

6. Next, use this space to write a psalm, poem, or free-flowing prose addressed to God, expressing your frustration and other emotions regarding this issue.

7. Connect to a local church, NGO, or other organization and explore opportunities for engagement on your issue. Whether it's a one-time visit to get your feet wet or it develops into a long-term partnership, seeing how a local NGO or faith-based organization combats this issue gives you a real-life experience. Take a minute to ask around in the group for recommendations, and do a bit of online research. If you live in a major city, there's a good chance that a social entrepreneurship center, such as "Impact Hub" (google it) exists with connections to your identified issue, or that a local church is already taking a stand against injustice on your issue.

    Add any notes here:

Cool Down Stage (15 minutes):

8. To wrap-up this exercise, take action right now by making a phone call or writing an email to make contact with the church or organization above.

9. Strengthen the action with accountability, choosing to surround yourself with two to three wise discerning voices to receive feedback on your plans, as well as follow-up with you. If possible, carry out action step 7 in community—with a group of people.
   Write down the names of those in your community or two to three voices here:

Prophetic Equipping Exercises

Equipping Exercise 5: Functioning Together as a Body

In this exercise we want to gather together for an open time with no fixed agenda, where we will learn what it looks like to function as a body underneath the headship of Christ. The text in Ephesians 4, discussed earlier in this book, is relevant here:

> Rather, speaking the truth in love, we are to grow up in every way into him who is the head, into Christ, from whom the whole body, joined and held together by every joint with which it is equipped, when each part is working properly, makes the body grow so that it builds itself up in love.
>
> Ephesians 4:15-16

We want to see how this can happen practically in a group of believers. For each part to be working properly, an understanding and emphasis of the priesthood of all believers is necessary, not as a theological statement but as a reality to be practiced:

> But you are a chosen race, a royal priesthood, a holy nation, a people for his own possession, that you may proclaim the excellencies of him who called you out of darkness into his marvelous light.
>
> 1 Peter 2:9

Because each one of us is a priest, each one can minister to the other.

Flowing out of the reality of the priesthood of all believers, this exercise should encompass a variety of spiritual gifts and by doing so will display the riches of Christ through his body. Consider these verses:

> Well, my brothers and sisters, let's summarize. When you meet together, one will sing, another will teach, another will tell some special revelation God has given, one will speak in tongues, and another will interpret what is said. But everything that is done must strengthen all of you.
>
> 1 Corinthians 14:26 NLT

It's likely you will see all five of the fivefold ministries present during this exercise—this will be a sweet time of *koinonia* (Greek: "fellowship"), shared life of the Spirit, as you enjoy Christ together. Get ready—this has the potential to be a powerful time of community, intimacy, peace, freedom, variety, spontaneity, love, and more!

SUGGESTED TIME: Minimum 3 hours (you'll be surprised how quickly the time goes by—you may decide to take even longer—but at least this amount of time is recommended)

SUPPLIES: Instruments or a device to play music

GROUP SETUP: A circle, reflecting the worship in heaven as seen in Revelation 4

GROUP LEADER PREPARATION: Set up a date and time to meet, ask all to be praying for this special time together, even fasting, and engage someone to lead worship

OBJECTIVES:

- To learn to work as a body under the headship of Christ
- To create an environment of mutual building up
- To create an open atmosphere to allow spiritual gifts to blossom

DIRECTIONS: *(Note: while numbered directions are listed here, this exercise more than any other will be fluid, and feel more like a "flow" rather than individual steps. Furthermore, in an effort to make the directions more tangible, notes from experience have been added.)*

Warm-Up Stage (15 minutes):

1. As people arrive and settle in, begin to share expectations for the time together. Why are you here? What are you looking forward to? What are you expecting from God?

   Experiential note: One participant shared: "My most vivid memory is that there was a hunger from everyone to meet with the Lord. There was a sense of anticipation that God was going to show up." And another, "There was a buzz in the room as people were arriving."

Working Stage (at least 2 hours 20 minutes):

2. Begin with live worship music for thirty to forty-five minutes. It can be as simple as an acoustic guitar. If live music isn't possible, choose some YouTube worship videos. Sing, worship, adore Jesus, and focus on his holiness and love. Let your problems melt away as you take your focus off yourself and get lost in

his presence. Confess things to the Lord if needed. This time is essential to building spiritual unity at a heart and spirit level.

> Experiential note: One time a person had the sense that our worship and prayers were "hitting the ceiling," so they turned to another person and shared that. The second person had that same sense, and so the two of them shared it with the larger group. A third person then stood up and said the Spirit had put something on his heart ... then he began a spontaneous rap about repentance! In consensus, the twenty-five people or so broke up into two groups by gender and spent time confessing to one another, seeking the Lord to remove any sin or thing that might be blocking their corporate worship. When they gathered back together, there was such a purity and holiness to the atmosphere, the worship nearly blew off the ceiling!

3. Continue with light worship music in the background and begin to simply share what touched you during the worship time. Look out for any reoccurring themes—this may be the direction the Head wants to move the body. Pay attention to any particularly difficult situations that are shared—these parts of the body may need ministering to individually as the rest of the body gathers around in prayer for them. This time is about connecting the body together "that there may be no division in the body, but that the members may have the same care for one another. If one member suffers, all suffer together; if one member is honored, all rejoice together" (1 Corinthians 12:25–26).

> Experiential note: One member sensed the weight of his life calling, and was face down on the floor sobbing, feeling burdened and ill-equipped for the journey. The rest of the members gathered around him, speaking ease and rest over him, as well as equipping, power, courage, and strength for the task ahead.

4. Continue in this flow of "one anothering." The New Testament is full of over fifty references where the believers gathered together and engaged in mutual edification: "love one another," "pray for one another," "carry one another's burdens," "encourage one another," "serve one another," "submit to one another," "forgive one another," "teach one another," etc.[54] Allow the space for people to share a Scripture, short teaching, or a song. The time should be organic and led by the Spirit. This may be challenging for those

---

54   For an overview of all the "one another" passages in the New Testament see Jeffrey Kanz, "All the 'one another' commands in the NT [infographic]," OverviewBible, March 9, 2014, https://overviewbible.com/one-another-infographic/ .

who are familiar with a more structured schedule or church service.

> Experiential note: Functioning as a body underneath the headship of Christ is not easy. We are so used to following a single leader, a human head. Yet it is possible. From one woman: "The Holy Spirit was able to lead because there was not a fixed agenda of what should happen." Another guy expressed, "The Holy Spirit was leading the meeting. Not one meeting was ever the same." And a third testimony: "The Holy Spirit was clearly leading our meetings, and we didn't need a leader as such, because each person operated in their gifting, or explored what their gifting could look like in its expression. I remember unity and humility in the group." You will observe this dynamic of the Holy Spirit's leadership in the "chain reactions" happening throughout the evening, such as the repentance chain reaction described above, after point two, or the experiential note below number five.

5. There may be times of silence during the time together. Just wait on the Lord. Embrace the stillness, God's presence, and his peace. "Be still and know that I am God" (Psalm 46:10). Silence may be a needed break, or a time when the Spirit will shift things to a different theme. Don't speak up simply out of discomfort of silence; but, if your heart is quickening and you sense the Spirit prompting you, do share what he has placed on your heart. There's a balance here of having the faith and boldness to open your mouth and speak, versus interrupting the peaceful stillness out of discomfort or awkwardness.

> Experiential note: "There was silence for what seemed like minutes. Yet it was peaceful, with no urge to be doing anything or going anywhere. Then a violin began to play sweet, melodic tunes that seemed to resonate deeply in people's souls. You could tell that individuals were moved by their facial expressions or light groans, but no one knew exactly why. Then, in the spur of the moment, one person had an interpretation for that specific melody!" Those words from the Lord through his body built up everyone in the room, and those it seemed to particularly impact were prayed for individually.

Cool Down Stage (25 minutes):

6. As things begin to wind down, someone will get a sense of when the time is up.[55] Begin to close by sharing short testimonies of what has happened in the time. These should be one-to-two minute thanksgivings,

---

55 The head, Jesus, speaks through his body and therefore it might be anyone within the group who gets the sense that it is time to close. This will then be confirmed by others in the body.

bringing awareness of how the Lord has encouraged, strengthened, brought clarity, direction, wisdom, healing, etc., through his body. The goal is not to fully digest everything, but process a bit as things are shared and to bring closure to the time together. This also builds up faith for the next gathering!

> Experiential note: One participant described her bliss: "I remember intense times of worship, holding hands in a circle and lifting up our King together. It wasn't forced; it just came and happened because we were all in awe of Jesus. It often felt like we were experiencing a heavenly reality, something we had never tasted before. I remember corporate repentance, as well as encouragement. I remember experiencing God like I never had before, him speaking to me like he had never done before, a desire for him more than I have ever tasted before … I remember I never wanted it to end, as it was the most freeing place I had ever been."

7. Have someone seal the wonderful things that have happened in the time together with a prayer.

Prophetic individuals are uniquely gifted by Jesus to creatively connect to and express the Father's heart, inspiring **faithfulness to God and justice in the world**.

6

The Evangelistic Exercises
Relating, Re-Gospeling, Reconciling

"The Son of Man came to seek and to save the lost" (Luke 19:10). This statement not only encapsulates the reason Jesus came but also succinctly explains evangelistic ministry. The focus is to seek out and save the lost. God's nature is inviting, pursuing, communicative, full of love and grace, saving, and redeeming. And so we can see that evangelism is not merely a ministry but is actually rooted in who God is. These characteristics shaped and formed Jesus, as well as the evangelistic ministry and individual gifting.

Jesus the Evangelist was the physical embodiment of the gospel, so while we commonly associate the term with the message we share, we mustn't forget that the gospel is a person. At the same time, the gospel, literally "good news," is also a spoken message about Jesus.

Jesus began his public ministry proclaiming the gospel, "The time is fulfilled, and the kingdom of God is at hand; repent and believe in the gospel" (Mark 1:15). His gospel was a "big gospel" referring to the whole gospel of the kingdom of God (read more about this in the bonus material at the back of the book), and this should therefore inform our gospel message. Jesus lived out the gospel in a variety of ways, setting an example for us. He was a master at initiating spiritual conversations by engaging people with questions; he performed signs and miracles so that people would believe in him; he boldly proclaimed the gospel of the kingdom; and he transformed the lives of many people—giving each a powerful story of their encounter. The following equipping activities will utilize many of these techniques.

As we read in the text of Ephesians 4, Jesus gave the gift of the evangelist to his body, the church. He gave some to be evangelists for the church, not just to share the good news but to equip others to share the good news. Therefore, there is an inward purpose of the evangelist as well, to "re-gospel" the church, keeping the gospel fresh, aflame, and accurate. And while Ephesians 4:11 makes it clear there are some who will mature into an equipping evangelist, we are *all* called to share our faith in some way, shape, or form. "Go into all the world and proclaim the gospel to the whole creation," Jesus told his disciples in Mark 16:15, a command that is passed on to us. When a church has a healthy and mature evangelistic culture, members know the gospel internally and are able to verbally share it with others. The church has a welcoming environment, where all—even outcasts of society—feel welcomed and accepted. The church will grow numerically, and the fresh inflow will invigorate the church, through testimonies of salvation, for example.

On an individual level, the evangelist's core burden is for those who do not know Jesus. Their heart breaks for the lost, and they find themselves comfortably in non-Christian circles. Theirs is a ministry of reconciliation, reconciling a lost son or daughter to their Father through Jesus, helping them understand that Jesus is "the way, the truth and the life. No one comes to the Father except through [him]" (John 14:6). They are usually extroverted with high emotional intelligence, able to relate well to people, and are uniquely gifted to steer conversations in such a way that leads to the gospel. They are constantly "re-gospeling," adjusting God's story or their story, so it makes sense to the culture, the person, and even the situation. Mature evangelists will not see people as projects, but rather as people with unique journeys and stories. They will do especially well to partner with teachers, who will continue discipling individuals and communities deeper in the Word, and with shepherds to include the individuals in community.

> **Evangelistic individuals** are uniquely gifted by Jesus to powerfully proclaim the good news of the gospel, inspiring **repentance and salvation**.

The following exercises will help everyone grow in awareness and application of evangelistic ministry.

Preview of evangelistic equipping exercises:

Equipping Exercise 1: Preparing and Praying Your Personal *Oikos*
Equipping Exercise 2: Active Listening and Spirit-led Questioning
Equipping Exercise 3: My Gospel Toolkit
Equipping Exercise 4: The Power of Your Story
Equipping Exercise 5: The 7 Signs in John

Evangelistic Equipping Exercises

Equipping Exercise 1: Preparing And Praying Your Personal *Oikos*

Salvation is a miracle. This inner transformation of someone's heart can only come about through the power of God through the Holy Spirit. While the following evangelistic activities are all worthwhile, nothing is more crucial than prayer. Through prayer, God releases his power to move the seemingly immovable, soften the hardest of hearts, and reach those farthest away. As we are seated with Christ in heavenly places, we lock arms with Jesus to partner with him in reaching a lost world. He chooses to use us as vessels through which he can reach those around us. Those people around us are the circles of influence we have, our *Oikos*, a Greek word in the New Testament referring to a relational network. These people are important to recognize, target, and pray for, as *you* may be the only Bible someone ever reads.

We see from the parable of the four soils in Mark 4 that the seed of the gospel only takes root and sprouts if it has good soil, void of rockiness and thorns, and protected from birds that snatch up the seed. As we seek to emulate Jesus as he "came to seek and to save the lost," we will be the most fruitful when we target those things in prayer, collaborating with God as much as possible for him to bring someone from the kingdom of darkness into the kingdom of light.

SUGGESTED TIME: 30 minutes
SUPPLIES: Paper and something to write with
GROUP SETUP: None
GROUP LEADER PREPARATION: None

OBJECTIVES:

- To identify people in your *oikos*
- To cultivate a regular prayer habit for those people
- To see people we know and love get saved!

DIRECTIONS:

Warm-Up Stage (5 minutes):

1. Pray and ask the Holy Spirit to move in power.

Working Stage (20 minutes):

2. Think about your own *oikos*. Use the chart below to fill in as many names as possible into each one of the categories.

Family	Friends	Co-workers	Neighbors	Other
EMMA	CHARLIE	TERRY	ANN	JERMAINE
NICOLA	JAMES	PAUL	DAVE	
Jimmy		MICHELLE	ALISON	
GARETH		JENNY	MATTHEW	
DEREK		RICHARD		
EILEEN		JON		
HENRY		JAMIE		
ANGELA				

3. As there are likely an abundance of names, ask the Holy Spirit to highlight just three names to focus on right now—people you have a lot of contact with or you expect to see this week. Write their names below.

EMMA, TERRY, GARETH

4. Pray for God to prepare their heart and draw them to himself by praying John 6:44:

"No one can come to me unless the Father who sent me draws him. And I will raise him up on the last day."

5. Pray for an open door to share Christ naturally by praying Colossians 4:2-6:

Continue steadfastly in prayer, being watchful in it with thanksgiving. At the same time, pray also for us, that God may open to us a door for the word, to declare the mystery of Christ, on account of which I am in prison—that I may make it clear, which is how I ought to speak. Walk in wisdom toward outsiders, making the best use of the time. Let your speech always be gracious, seasoned with salt, so that you may know how you ought to answer each person.

6. Pray for yourself, for boldness when you encounter them in that moment by praying the following:

And now, Lord, look upon their threats and grant to your servants to continue to speak your word with all boldness

Acts 4:29

For I am not ashamed of the gospel, for it is the power of God for salvation to everyone who believes, to the Jew first and also to the Greek.

Romans 1:16

Cool Down Stage (5 minutes):

7. Commit to praying for these three people daily for a few minutes in the morning.[56]

8. Build in five minutes of praying for these three people each time you meet with other Christians.

9. Share updates of your "three people" the next time you meet—you will be amazed how God works! Use the space below to write down any updates.

---

56   Alternate Scriptures to pray to add variety in the future: John 16:8–10, 2 Corinthians 4:4, Colossians 1:13, Mark 4:20.

Evangelistic Equipping Exercises

Equipping Exercise 2: Active Listening and Spirit-Led Questioning

In this equipping exercise you will learn some simple but powerful questions to ask, as well as gaining the opportunity to practice active listening. The adage from John Cassis applies here: "People don't care how much you know until they know how much you care." That's why this exercise is key for evangelistic equipping. To listen is to care. To care is to show love. While many assume evangelism is only for extroverts, this exercise is especially beneficial for introverts that find sharing their faith difficult, as asking simple but powerful questions directs the other person to do the talking and opens doors to deeper issues.

Doug Pollock, in his book *GodSpace,* focuses on questioning and listening in evangelism. With a balance of Spirit-led listening and Spirit-led questioning, the conversation is automatically steered towards spiritual things, since all deep conversations must end with God.[57] An opportune moment to share the gospel often comes after the person has talked for a while, then asks what you think, where you stand, or what you believe. It is in those moments you will be able to share a similar experience or share something you have read that morning in the Word that fits perfectly. Using that as a bridge, you can tailor the gospel to what they have shared. "Let your speech always be gracious, seasoned with salt, so that you may know how you ought to answer each person" (Colossians 4:6). We are not to water the gospel down, but, like Paul, to relate to others in such a way that we "become all things to all people, that by all means I might save some" (1 Corinthians 9:22).

SUGGESTED TIME: 40 minutes
SUPPLIES: None
GROUP SETUP: Triads
GROUP LEADER PREPARATION: None

---

57   Doug Pollock, *GodSpace: Where Spiritual Conversations Happen Naturally* (Lifetree, 2009).

OBJECTIVES:

- To hone active listening skills so as to show love, be patient, and wait for the open door to share the gospel
- To see people we know and love get saved

DIRECTIONS:

Warm-Up Stage (5 minutes):

1. Form groups of three: one person is the active listener, one person is the speaker, and one person is the observer. If there are only two people available, then disregard the observer. With a total timeframe of thirty minutes, you should rotate every ten minutes to allow each person to experience each role. Allow one or two minutes of constructive feedback within each ten-minute rotation (explained in step 3).

Working Stage (30 minutes):

2. The active **listener** begins with a question, and proceeds to listen actively by affirming with non-verbal body language and from time-to-time reflecting back what the speaker has said with short summarizing phrases.

   List of sample questions:
   - Where are you from?
   - What do you do for a living? Why did you choose that profession?
   - What are you really passionate about?
   - What three things are most important to you in life? And why?
   - As you've watched or read the news, what conclusions have you drawn about the nature of humanity?
   - Have you ever had an experience where you felt the presence of evil? Have you ever had an experience where you felt the presence of God? Would you like to? (You can offer to pray with them at the end of the conversation for them to sense God's presence).
   - What do you believe about God?
   - Who is Jesus to you?
   - What concerns you most when you think about your future?
   - Do you ever find yourself doing the very things you don't want to do, or not doing the things you

really want to do? If so, what do you attribute this to? Have you ever found anything to set you free from this cycle?

- I'm convinced everyone's on a spiritual journey in life. Where are you on your spiritual journey?
- If you could know for certain how to be at peace with God and spend eternity with him, would you want to know how?[58]

3. Once the conversation comes to an end, the **observer** gives constructive feedback to both persons. In addition, the **speaker** should give feedback on how well "listened to" they felt, e.g., "Was the person genuinely interested in me? Would I go away from this conversation feeling loved?"

Jot any notes down in the space below.

---

58   A list of Pollock's 99 questions from *GodSpace* can be found here: Doug Pollock, "99 Wondering Questions That Could Work for You," https://www.cru.org/content/dam/cru/communities/campus/99-wondering-questions.pdf .

Rotate so that all three people experience each role.

Cool Down Stage (5 minutes):

4.   What are you taking away from this exercise? Did it give you a new perspective on what evangelism could look like? Which of the questions is your favorite that you can take with you and try to use in the next few days? Write a few reflections below, then share them with the group to close.

Evangelistic Equipping Exercises

Equipping Exercise 3: My Gospel Toolkit

There are many great ways of sharing the gospel, using different tools that enable the believer to share their faith. The method is not necessarily important. What's important is the believer grasping the gospel in their own head and heart, and the gospel going forth in some way, shape, or form. It's helpful to have a toolkit from which to draw from, so that in any situation the right "tool" can be chosen. The power of the gospel will accomplish its work, no matter how it is shared—that's the Holy Spirit's job. Therefore, we simply share unashamedly, planting and watering. God brings the growth (1 Corinthians 3:6).

SUGGESTED TIME: 60 minutes for the tool of choice
SUPPLIES: 3 sheets of blank paper per person
GROUP SETUP: In 2s or 3s
GROUP LEADER PREPARATION: A thorough understanding of each of the tools (including watching the videos listed in the exercises)

OBJECTIVES:

By choosing one of the gospel tools below, either (A) designed for beginners, (B) an intermediate tool, or (C) an advanced tool, each person and the collective group is enabled:

- To grow in awareness of the gospel
- To grow in application of sharing the gospel

(A) Beginner: "Sharing THE FOUR Gospel"

This is a simple tool to help explain the gospel using four simple symbols.[59] It can be used anywhere and explained in just a few minutes.

DIRECTIONS:

Warm-Up Stage (10 minutes):

1. Pair up and spend time together looking up each one of the verses below to familiarize yourself with them.

Working Stage Part I (20 minutes):

2. Take turns sharing THE FOUR:

i. **God loves me.** 1 John 4:16; John 3:16; Jeremiah 29:11
ii. **I live apart from God.** Romans 3:23; Romans 6:23
iii. **Jesus gave everything for me.** Romans 5:8; 2 Corinthians 5:21; John 3:16
iv. **Will I choose to follow Jesus?** John 1:12; John 14:6; Romans 10:9

3. Provide feedback to one another.

4. Switch and share with a new partner.

---

59   Logo and content used by permission from Raphael Marti THE FOUR Project Leader, Switzerland, via email to author on July 26, 2016. To learn more or watch video clips associated with The Four, check out https://thefour.com/ .

5. As you become more and more comfortable, it would be great to have a future goal to memorize one of the verses listed above for each of THE FOUR for your personal benefit and to be able to weave them into your explanation, especially for times when you don't have a Bible available. Write out the verse you'd like to memorize here:

Working Stage Part II and Cool Down Stage (30 minutes):

6. After learning this tool, practicing it together, and a time of prayer, go out to a park or similar and share THE FOUR with two people, then regroup to close with testimonies. We only truly learn when we step out of our comfort zone and have a go!

Note: If the person you talk to wants to learn more, go through each of the Scriptures individually with them. Have them read the verse aloud, and ask what their understanding is of it. If something is unclear, explain to them what it means. This follows the example we read in Acts 8:29–31, 35:

> And the Spirit said to Philip, "Go over and join this chariot." So Philip ran to him and heard him reading Isaiah the prophet and asked, "Do you understand what you are reading?" And he said, "How can I, unless someone guides me?" And he invited Philip to come up and sit with him ... Then Philip opened his mouth, and beginning with this Scripture he told him the good news about Jesus.

(B) Intermediate: "The 3 Circles Gospel"

This 3 Circles tool incorporates the power of storytelling into sharing the gospel. You will learn a simple sketch of three circles that explains i. the world of brokenness we live in, ii. God's original design, and iii. Jesus, whom God used to redeem the world itself and individual lives. This simple formulation of the gospel is often used to begin a dialogue with people. It's best used over lunch or sitting at a coffee shop and can easily be drawn on a napkin or extra piece of notebook paper in about three minutes.

DIRECTIONS:

Warm-Up Stage (10 minutes):

1. If there is an individual in the group who is familiar with the 3 Circles, they should teach it to everyone else, sketching it out as they go. If there is no one available to do this, you can watch a video explanation on Vimeo: https://vimeo.com/140957422.

Working Stage Part I (30 minutes):

2. Have the same person (if applicable) sketch the 3 Circles again and have each group member sketch it step-by-step in the space below.

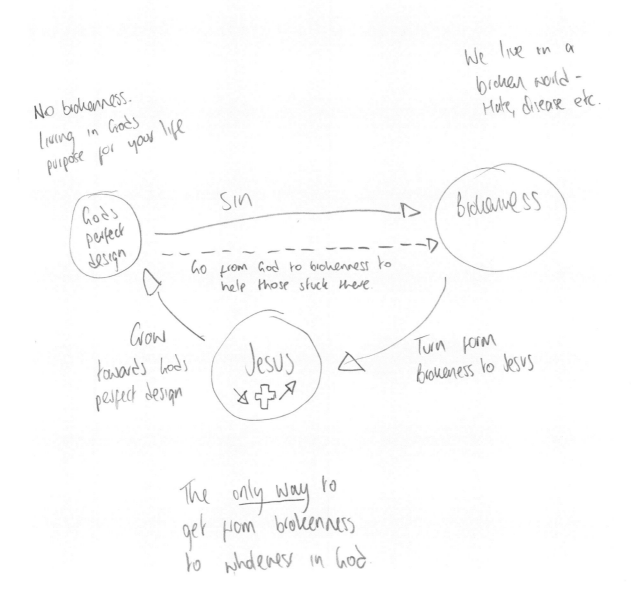

3. Pair up in twos and practice sketching the 3 Circles once for each other in the space below.

4. Find a new partner and practice sketching the 3 Circles a second time in the space below, aiming to keep it under three minutes.

Working Stage Part II and Cool Down Stage (20 minutes):

5.   After learning this tool, practicing it together, and a time of prayer, go out and share with two people, then regroup to close with testimonies. Take some blank sheets of paper with you. We only truly learn when we step out of our comfort zone and have a go!

(C) Advanced: "The Full Gospel of the Kingdom"

For those who are familiar with the first two tools already, or who have taken time to master them, this advanced option is for you! Jesus' gospel was a gospel of the kingdom—good news about the King's rule and reign. Typically the gospel is presented as salvation from personal sins and an individual ticket to heaven. This is true and good, but the gospel is even bigger! In this exercise, you will focus on composing and sharing a larger, fuller gospel message: the gospel of the kingdom.

DIRECTIONS:

Warm-Up Stage (10 minutes):

1.   Start by reading the section "His Pulse in You—the Gospel of the King(dom)" (page 229).

Working Stage Part I (20 minutes):

2.   Choose seven key words/phrases from that text to give you anchor points, seven accompanying verses, and draw a simple symbol next to it as a memory trigger. Fill them out in the chart below. A few have been done for you to give you a jump start, and a few are completely open to fill in other parts that you feel would enrich your communication of the gospel of the kingdom.

Phrase	Verse	Symbol
The King pre-existed	John 1:1–3	
The King and kingdom are foreshadowed (OT)		
The King is coming again		

Working Stage Part II (25 minutes):

3. Practice sharing the gospel of the kingdom verbally, using your chart and notes.

4. Practice sharing the gospel of the kingdom visually by drawing the symbols in the space below and explaining the symbols one by one verbally.

Provide feedback to one another. Jot down any feedback you receive in the space below.

Cool Down Stage (5 minutes):

5. Close with prayer for the gospel of the kingdom to sink more into your heart and head, and for an opportunity to share it this week with someone who has never heard this good news.

Evangelistic Equipping Exercises

Equipping Exercise 4: The Power of Your Story

The steps and tips in this exercise will help you prepare and tell a three-minute version of your testimony with sincerity, impact, and clarity, illustrating the power of what God has done in your life. Realize first and foremost, that no matter what your life has looked like, there is power in your testimony! Revelation 12:11 says we overcome our enemy "by the blood of the Lamb and by the word of [our] testimony." In this exercise, an effective three-point approach will be used to communicate your personal testimony in three minutes. The outline focuses on three stages of your life: 1. before you trusted Christ, 2. how you surrendered to him, and 3. the difference since you've been walking with him.[60]

SUGGESTED TIME: 60 minutes
SUPPLIES: A sheet of paper and colored pens or pencils
GROUP SETUP: Triads
GROUP LEADER PREPARATION: None

OBJECTIVES:

- To believe that each person has a powerful story because the gospel of salvation is itself powerful
- To learn how to share your story in three minutes or less

DIRECTIONS:

Warm-Up Stage (10 minutes):

1. **Spend Time in Thought Preparation**
   There are a few things to consider before you start writing your story. If you like, read Acts 26:9–20 for

---

60   Mary Fairchild, "How to Write Your Christian Testimony," About Religion, last modified February 8, 2016, http://christianity.about.com/od/testimonies/a/howtotestimony.htm .

a great example of Paul's life story. Think about your life before you met the Lord. What was going on in your life leading up to your conversion? What problems or needs were you facing at the time? How did your life change after that? You will elaborate on each of these questions in the next steps, but jot some initial thoughts down in the space below. Thank Jesus for saving you.

- Always knew about Jesus, it didn't become personal until I experienced the holy spirit and God speaking to me on a retreat holiday.

- I wasn't facing problems

- My life changed because I started to look for God instead of just exist knowing that he existed.

  ↳ I didn't learn about Gods character and who I am until recus.

Working Stage Part I (20 minutes):

2. **Start with a Simple Three-Point Outline**

i. **Before**: Simply tell what your life was like before you surrendered to Christ. What were you searching for before coming to know Christ? What was the key problem, emotion, situation, or attitude you were dealing with? What motivated you? What were your actions? How did you try to satisfy your inner needs? (Examples of inner needs are loneliness, fear of death, insecurity. Possible ways to fill those needs include work, money, drugs, relationships, sports, sex.) Jot your thoughts down in the space below.

It was a normal life. I wasn't searching for God. I already knew he was there I just didn't know what It meant for me.

ii. **How**: How were you converted? Simply tell the events and circumstances that caused you to consider Christ as the solution to your searching. Take time to identify the steps that brought you to the point of trusting Christ. Where were you? What was happening at the time? What people or problems influenced your decision? Jot your thoughts down in the space below.

It was at revive we had a well-done youth tent, good worship, that allowed me to see God. ~~People prayed for me~~ I went forward for prayer, though I don't know why. That's when I knew that God loves me, and It made me want to find out more about him.

iii. **Since**: How has your life in Christ made a difference? How has his forgiveness impacted you? How have your thoughts, attitudes, and emotions changed? Share how Christ is meeting your needs and what a relationship with him means to you now. Jot some thoughts down in the space below.

Since then I started reading my bible and praying regularly, I joined the worship team and saw God in all of my life. I chased after my passion for music and God.

(I think I've lost that a little in recent months)

I've struggled to make time for God since having a child. Life is hard, but I know God is graceful, and I know he knows I love him.

3. **Important Tips to Remember**

- **Stick to the point**. Your conversion and new life in Christ should be the main points.
- **Be specific**. Include events, genuine feelings, and personal insights that clarify your main point. This makes your testimony tangible—something others can relate to.
- **Be current**. Tell what is happening in your life with God now, today.
- **Be honest**. Don't exaggerate or dramatize your life for effect. The simple truth of what God has done in your life is all the Holy Spirit needs to convict others of their sin and convince them of his love and grace.
- **Stay away from "Christianese" phrases**. Foreign, "churchy" words can alienate listeners and readers and keep them from identifying with your life.

Working Stage Part II (20 minutes):

4. **Practice Sharing**

In your group of three, take turns sharing your story in three minutes or less. After each person shares, ask permission to give them feedback. Then everyone should find a new group and practice sharing a second time. Use the space below to write any personal feedback you receive:

Cool Down Stage (10 minutes):

5. **Set Goals**

Think of two to three non-Christian people you can share your story with this week. They could be people on your list from Equipping Exercise 1 or new people you encounter. One strategy could be a simple phone call to a friend, "Hey, I'm doing this homework assignment for a training I'm taking, and I was wondering if you could help me for five minutes? I'm supposed to share my spiritual story with two to three people and get their feedback. Can I share it with you over the phone and get your feedback?"

Write down the names of people you will contact and when you aim to share your story with them.

6. **Pray and Commission One Another**

Spend a few minutes closing the time in prayer, praying for one another for boldness to share your story and for natural opportunities to do so. Lay a hand on the person next to you and commission them to be an ambassador for Christ!

Evangelistic Equipping Exercises

Equipping Exercise 5: The 7 Signs in John

As you increasingly share the good news with others, you will discover people who are not interested at all in the gospel. For these people, the goal is to leave them feeling loved and to commit to praying that God softens their heart. There will also be those who seem desperate and are ready to accept the gospel immediately. Fantastic! Then there will be those with whom you speak who are curious, not ready to commit, but open to learning more ... this tool is for them. The 7 Signs in John are seven accounts of seven of Jesus' miracles ("signs") recorded in the Gospel of John. Jesus performed each of these signs explicitly so that a person may believe that he is the Christ, and that by believing they may have life in his name (John 20:31). The concept is to meet with a person regularly, e.g., once a week, and look at the seven signs together. Ideally, the short passage is read once every day in preparation for meeting up. The time is then spent engaging with the questions listed on page 157, and any other questions the participant may have. This is known as the "Discovery Bible Study" method and it re-frames evangelism in the context of discipleship, as the participant is already being discipled in the process, even though they are not yet saved.

SUGGESTED TIME: 60 minutes
SUPPLIES: None
GROUP SETUP: Pairs
GROUP LEADER PREPARATION: None

OBJECTIVES:

- To become familiar with the Discovery Bible Study method
- To guide the person you're meeting with to get to know Jesus "face-to-face" in a personal way by looking together at key Bible texts and answering questions to grasp key points
- To see people we know believe in Jesus and get saved

DIRECTIONS:

Warm-Up Stage (10 minutes):

1. Begin with a prayer, honoring Jesus that he "is the Christ, the Son of God, and that by believing you may have life in his name" (John 20:31). Thank him for the miracles/signs he did to prove this, and that they have been written so that others may believe in him. Pray that getting equipped in this exercise will lead to someone choosing to believe and follow Jesus.

2. Pair up for a role play. Choose who will be the Christian facilitating and who will be the person who's seeking.

Working Stage (45 minutes):

3. Role play a conversation ... "I notice you're curious about spiritual things and specifically who Jesus is. Would you be open to meeting up for coffee sometime for one hour and looking at Jesus together?" (This makes the barrier to entry very low and removes fear.)

4. Continue the role play and imagine you are now meeting up for that coffee.

   After a bit of small talk, you introduce the idea of the first sign in John 2:1–11. "Shall we look at it together?" (See "The Seven Signs of John" on page 157 for the full list of Bible passages and questions to ask after reading each one. It's probably wise not to give a copy of this to the participant, lest they feel like they are stuck in a "program.")

5. Read John 2:1–11.

6. Go through the questions on page 157 to ask about the story.

7. Answer any other questions the participant may have.

Cool Down Stage (5 minutes):

8. At the end, present the idea of meeting up again. Here you can mention that there are actually seven signs/miracles that Jesus did specifically to show who he was. "Would you like to check out the second one?" Take it slow, step-by-step.

9. Throughout the week, commit to pray for the person every day as there will be a fierce spiritual battle going on trying to prevent them from getting into the Word and, ultimately, believing in Jesus.

> **Evangelistic individuals** are uniquely gifted by Jesus to powerfully proclaim the good news of the gospel, inspiring **repentance and salvation**.

THE 7 SIGNS IN JOHN

But these are written so that you may believe that Jesus is the Christ, the Son of God, and that by believing you may have life in his name.

—John 20:31

1. Changing the Water to Wine — John 2:1–11
2. Healing the Official's Son — John 4:46–54
3. The Invalid of Bethesda — John 5:1–18
4. The Feeding of the 5,000 — John 6:5–14
5. Jesus Walking on Water — John 6:16–21 (25–35)
6. Jesus Heals a Man Born Blind — John 9:1–41
7. The Resurrection of Lazarus — John 11:17–46

Questions to ask about each story:

- What does this story say about people?
- What does this story say about Jesus?
- What does this story say about you?
- What are you going to do about it?
- Who needs to hear this story?

Neil Cole, "7 Signs in John," used by permission. For more background about this tool, see the article: "Seven Signs in John: a Simple Process for Evangelism and Starting Churches," CMA Resources, April 4, 2010. http://cmaresources.org/article/seven-signs-in-john .

7

The Shepherding Exercises
Connecting, Caring, Creating Community

Probably the most well-known of the five gifts of Jesus, the pastor/shepherd's primary concern as *poimen* (the original Greek) is shepherding the sheep. The imagery of shepherding derives from Jesus in Psalm 23 and John 10:11, "I am the Good Shepherd. The good shepherd lays down his life for the sheep." Shepherds sacrificially lay down their life to serve the sheep. Taking Psalm 23 into consideration, the Good Shepherd provides and protects, makes us lie down in green pastures, leads us beside still waters, and restores our soul. Additionally, he leads us in paths of righteousness for the sake of the Lord's name. As with all five gifts, Jesus is our example and models how this gifting should be expressed.

Christ has given some specific people a large measure of the gift of shepherding, and they use that to shepherd/pastor a local church body. However, we are all called to emulate the chief Shepherd and care for one another, as 1 Corinthians 12:25 expresses, "the members may have the same care one for another." Moreover, Galatians 6:2 exhorts us to, "Bear one another's burdens." Shepherds use their gifting to create an atmosphere of connection, care, and community.

When mature shepherding is occurring throughout a church body, there is healthy community—deep relationships are cultivated, and the family of God is beautifully demonstrated. The church will also be emotionally mature, as people will be able to look below the surface of their own soul into the roots of the issues they are facing, as well as set healthy boundaries, deal with grief and loss, break the power of past wounds or sins, and slow down to maintain healthy life rhythms.[61] Emotional health, wholeness, reconciliation, and peacemaking will lead to peace and unity among the flock. Neil Cole makes an interesting point regarding the scope of the gift:

> On average, a shepherd can adequately care for 70 to 100 people [...] A growing and maturing congregation creates a need for many shepherds. Though all five gifts must be present and active for a church to be healthy, we do not need equal numbers of every gift [...] We need more shepherds not because the role is more important than the others, but simply because the limited scope of the gift requires more gifted hands on deck to fulfill the mission of the church.[62]

Shepherd-hearted people can often be found working in non-church-staff vocations as counselors, social workers, psychologists, nurses, within human resources, or other such similar roles.

Shepherding individuals are uniquely gifted by Jesus to care for the soul and create connections, inspiring **community and healing**.

The following equipping activities will help stimulate a shepherd's heart, growing in awareness and application of this gift.

Preview of shepherding equipping exercises:

Equipping Exercise 1: Emulating Jesus as the Good Shepherd
Equipping Exercise 2: Creating a Life Timeline to Share
Equipping Exercise 3: It's Game Time!
Equipping Exercise 4: Foot Washing
Equipping Exercise 5: From Shame to Freedom

---

61   These principles are mentioned in Peter Scazzero, *The Emotionally Healthy Church, Updated and Expanded Edition: A Strategy for Discipleship That Actually Changes Lives* (Michigan: Zondervan, 2015). This is an excellent resource to refer to in terms of shepherding in emotionally healthy spirituality.
62   Cole with Kaak, Helfer, Baker and Waken. *Primal Fire*, 195.

Shepherding Equipping Exercises

Equipping Exercise 1: Emulating Jesus as the Good Shepherd

SUGGESTED TIME: 50 minutes
SUPPLIES: Bibles or printout of Psalm 23 and John 10
GROUP SETUP: Circle of chairs so that people are face-to-face
GROUP LEADER PREPARATION: None

OBJECTIVES:

- To create an awareness of Jesus as our shepherd
- To begin to create a healthy group dynamic where everyone feels comfortable sharing
- To emulate Jesus as our role model by serving others

DIRECTIONS:

Warm-Up Stage (15 minutes):

1. Have a volunteer read Psalm 23 once out loud for the group; then take time for each person to read it individually, in silence.

2. Who do you know who personally embodies Psalm 23? In what ways do they do this? Jot a few notes down here and then share with the group.

Working Stage (25 minutes):

3. Looking at Jesus as the perfect Shepherd in Psalm 23, what are some of his characteristics? Write them in the space below.

    Patient
    Father figure
    challenging
    people/relational interests.

Which ones do you most admire?

Which ones would you like to grow in?

What practical steps can you take to apply this to your life?

Looking at Jesus as the Good Shepherd in John 10:1–21, what are some of his characteristics?

What do verses 11–15 tell us about the Good Shepherd? How could you practically live this out?

Cool Down Stage (10 minutes):

4. The Good Shepherd sacrificially laid down his life to serve the sheep. In our day and age, the most valuable resource we have is time. Practice servant shepherding by sacrificing time for someone inside the group. To do this, have everyone think of a task they need to do this week that takes approximately one hour (for example, grocery shopping, yard work, running an errand, organizing a project ... you can get creative; be honest about your needs!). Write your task on a small sheet of paper with your name and phone number, fold it in half, and exchange all the papers randomly. Contact the person within twenty-four hours to ask them when would be the best time to do the task if it's schedule dependent. (If you want an extra challenge, write to or call someone *outside* the group who is *not* a believer and explain the exercise and that your homework is to do this for someone ... ask them what you can do for them this week.)

Shepherding Equipping Exercises

Equipping Exercise 2: Creating a Life Timeline to Share

Healthy, mature shepherds create community in such a way that good relationships are formed and the sheep feel connected and cared for. A key component to bring about depth in community is to create a safe place where people can show their weaknesses, be vulnerable, and receive healing in their soul.

What does a safe place look like? The foundation that needs to be established to enable people to feel secure and open up is an atmosphere where all are attentive, present in the moment, and patient. An essential element is therefore active listening—not advice giving. In this exercise, we want to learn what it feels like to share personal things from our life timeline with other people, even if we don't know them so well yet, as well as practice giving undivided attention as others share their own timelines, giving them a sense of security.

SUGGESTED TIME: 60 minutes (including a bit of buffer)
SUPPLIES: Paper and pencils for each person (ideally colored pencils or markers)
GROUP SETUP: Face-to-face, conducive for sharing
GROUP LEADER PREPARATION: None

OBJECTIVES:

- To personally reflect on the grand overview of your life by zooming out and recognizing how distinct events in your life have shaped and formed you as part of God's plan for you, working all things together for good (Romans 8:28)
- To practice actively listening to others
- To be intentional about going deeper in forming community by sharing highs and lows of your life

DIRECTIONS:

Warm-Up Stage (5 minutes):

1. Think of one person in your life—could be recent or long ago—who has influenced you positively and how? Write your thoughts down in one or two sentences in the space below.

Charlie.
Went through his divorce still looking at Jesus.
Changed his life and still kept Jesus at the centre.
He was still real and was affected by the whole thing, but now is in a great place because of Jesus.

Working Stage Part I (15 minutes):

2. Draw your life story as a timeline on the template arrow provided on page 168. Draw hash marks on your timeline at five key events that impacted you. These can be positive or negative experiences. Write key words or phrases or draw pictures *above* the positive experiences regarding why they impacted you, and how God used them to shape and form you. Similarly, write key words or phrases or draw pictures *below* the negative experiences regarding why they impacted you, and how God used them to shape and form you.

3. Draw two hash marks on your timeline at two points in the future that you hope or expect to happen. Write key words around those hash marks.

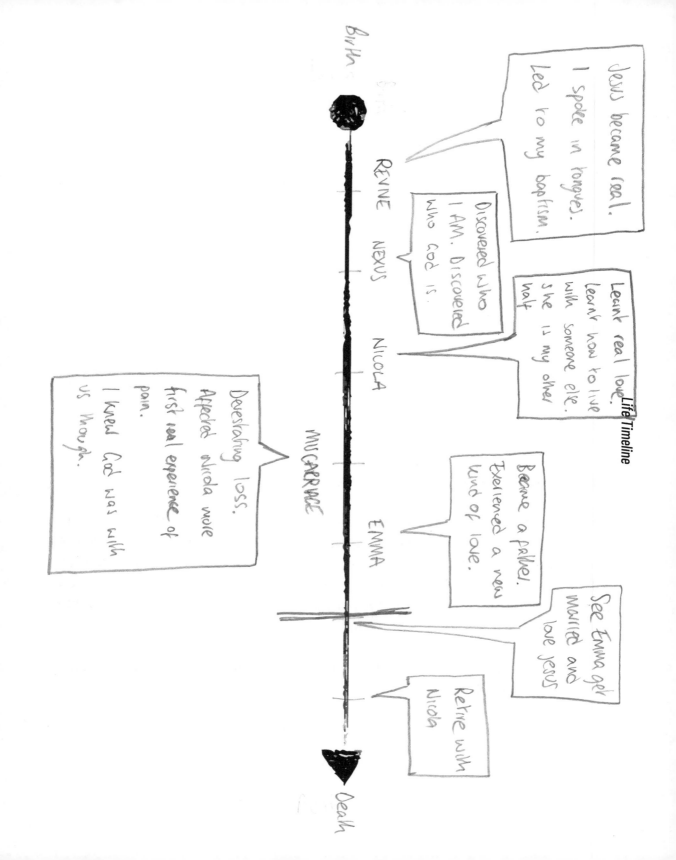

Working Stage Part II (30 minutes):

4. Share your key events with the group. Depending on size of group, sharing length will vary; it's important that each person gets equal time to share. If the group is quite large, then dividing into subgroups of four is helpful. It is also helpful here to appoint a moderator who keeps track of the time.

5. After an individual shares their timeline, listeners in the group can summarize what they have heard to promote active listening (for example, what touched them) or ask questions, yet should refrain from analyzing someone's life or giving them unsolicited advice.

Cool Down Stage (5 minutes):

6. Think of one person in the group whose Life Timeline you could particularly relate to? In what way could you relate? (Keep in mind that, statistically, not everyone will have a personal connection with another person; therefore, don't take it personally if no one chooses your timeline).

7. What are you taking away from this exercise in general? Write your thoughts below.

Shepherding Equipping Exercises

Equipping Exercise 3: It's Game Time!

Life can be tough. It can be very stressful and, at times, very painful. It's crucial we take time to rest and to have fun. Work is often very serious, and therefore it's good to lighten up. The Bible tells us, "A joyful heart is good medicine, but a crushed spirit dries up the bones" (Proverbs 17:22). A fun card game or board game with brothers and sisters in Christ can provide a light-hearted atmosphere that relieves stress and, at the same time, build relationships towards community. The goal is not just to hang out, but to have Christ-centered fellowship. The competition and camaraderie found in playing games together help foster community and create communal experiences to look back upon. Communities in Christ that play together stay together! If the weather is nice, and the group is so inclined, something more active like doubles ping-pong or Ultimate Frisbee are great options.

SUGGESTED TIME: 60 minutes
SUPPLIES: A deck of cards or a board game, light snacks
GROUP SETUP: According to game directions
GROUP LEADER PREPARATION: Think of a few card games or board games ahead of time as options, and have snacks on hand or delegate for someone to bring some

OBJECTIVES:

- To create an atmosphere of connection and community rooted in Christ
- To relax, laugh, and have fun!

DIRECTIONS:

Warm-Up Stage (15 minutes):

1. After a short time of fellowship over snacks, vote on which game to play if one hasn't been chosen already.

2. Explain the plan or directions of the game *and* the why behind it (intro above).

Playing Stage (40 minutes):

3. Start ...
4. Finish.

Cool Down Stage (5 minutes):

5. That's it—not many directions since the goal for this exercise is just relaxing and having fun. Reflect on this statement from the introduction to this exercise and jot your thoughts in the space below. *The competition and camaraderie found in playing games together help foster community and create communal experiences to look back upon.*

If you're really up for a challenge, throw a theme party! This *really* builds community as people get dressed up according to the theme, and it allows people to get a little out of character and be goofy. Specific theme ideas can be found easily online. Recommended framework: some food, music, and a relaxed program of team-based games.

Shepherding Equipping Exercises

Equipping Exercise 4: Foot Washing

This will be a very challenging exercise for some. You may not be keen to engage with this and may even want to interject, like Peter, "You shall never wash my feet!" Yet if you go through with this exercise, it will be very rewarding. The saying "don't knock it until you try it" is applicable here! Foot washing was certainly a more common occurrence when Jesus performed it 2,000 years ago, but of course he did it for a number of reasons, including to set an example for us to follow: "Now that I, your Lord and Teacher, have washed your feet, you also should wash one another's feet. I have set you an example that you should do as I have done for you" (John 13:14–15 NIV).

The foot washing recorded in John 13 happened just before the Feast of the Passover, when lambs were sacrificed to *cover up* the sins of Israel. Shortly afterwards, Jesus allowed himself to be sacrificed *to take away* the past, present, and future sins of the whole world. There is a lot of rich theology that could be unpacked from this passage, but that is beyond the scope of this exercise. A few chapters earlier, in John 10:11, Jesus described himself as "the good shepherd," going on to say, "The good shepherd lays down his life for the sheep." He demonstrated this sacrificial love prior to his crucifixion by performing a duty normally designated for a slave: washing the disciples' feet. Although his identity is esteemed as Lord and Teacher, he stoops down and humbly serves those who are following him. This is true leadership at its best. This is the mission that Jesus extends to us for the world, to humbly serve others in love.

Whether 2,000 years ago or today, it's very humbling to wash someone else's feet. It is also humbling to be the recipient of foot washing. Both positions can be somewhat uncomfortable. I guess that's how the disciples felt having Jesus wash their feet; and yet, just consider for a moment the extreme discomfort Jesus experienced as he was brutally beaten and as sharp nails were driven through his wrists and feet on the cross, just a few days later.

The challenge has been extended: a little discomfort for an opportunity to grow in humility, selflessness, servanthood, and love. Will you accept it?

SUGGESTED TIME: 35 minutes

SUPPLIES: Per pair – 1 large basin or Rubbermaid container filled 1/3 full with warm water and a bit of soap, or alternatively, a pool or river; 1 hand towel per pair for drying; some quiet background music while washing feet

GROUP SETUP: Pairs

GROUP LEADER PREPARATION: Bring a Bible, along with the supplies listed above

OBJECTIVES:

- To put our faith into action by following Jesus' example
- To experience what it's like to serve humbly
- To grow in our faith in the shepherd aspects of love, care, servanthood, humility, and selflessness

DIRECTIONS:

Warm-Up Stage (15 minutes):

1. Read John 13:1–20 for context.

Working Stage (5–10 minutes):

2. Prepare by partnering up and taking off shoes and socks. Due to the intimacy of this exercise, it's suggested to keep men with men and women with women.

3. Slowly wash one person's feet, cupping water over them to rinse. Don't feel pressured to fill the air with words; silence is okay. Alternatively, you can pray for the person while washing their feet.

4. Take the hand towel and dry their feet.

5. Switch.

Cool Down Stage (5-7 minutes):

6. Take a few minutes to silently reflect by jotting down some thoughts and feelings in the space below as you process.

7. For those who feel comfortable sharing, share with the group how the experience was for you.

8. End with a closing prayer.

Shepherding Equipping Exercises

Equipping Exercise 5: From Shame to Freedom

Do you have low self-esteem, feel worthless or exhausted? Or maybe you feel you can't be yourself for fear of being exposed. Wouldn't it be great to experience more freedom in your soul? Imagine what it would be like to bring things from your past into the light and be wholly accepted and loved. This is our Father's desire for us: to experience life to the fullest as wholly accepted children of our heavenly Father and to be free, living life audaciously in the light.

Why is dealing with shame so important? Generally speaking, shame often blocks our connection with God and others, therefore hindering our spiritual health and growth, as well as preventing us from forming authentic relationships. According to Steven R. Tracy in his book *Mending the Soul,* "Shame is a deep, painful sense of inadequacy and personal failure based on the inability to live up to a standard of conduct—one's own or one imposed by others."[63] Shame is a powerful evil force intended to warp our identity, as it disfigures God's character and our perception of ourselves being made in his image, as well as perverting God's grace, so that we feel ineligible to receive it.

Shame is different from conviction, and can be further clarified using the terms "healthy shame" and "toxic shame." In a healthy sense, conviction arising from healthy shame drives us *to* God, as the Holy Spirit makes us aware of our sin and gives us hope for redemption through Jesus. Toxic shame, on the other hand, drives us *away* from God, making us want to hide from him for fear of punishment. We also experience a lack of hope, as we feel unworthy of forgiveness and fear the real us may be exposed. And so we hide who we really are. This toxic shame can come from something we feel guilty about, and it can also originate from an incident that we are not guilty of, such as abuse.

> But if we walk in the light, as he is in the light, we have fellowship with one another.
>
> 1 John 1:7a

Hiding hinders authentic fellowship with our heavenly Father and with other believers, and ultimately, it hinders healing from the Lord. Thus, the key to overcoming shame is more than simply learning to love and accept oneself; it is to discern God's perspective on one's shame and

---

63   Steven R. Tracy, *Mending the Soul: Understanding and Healing Abuse* (Michigan: Zondervan: 2008), 74.

guilt, and to let his perspective drive and reshape one's thoughts, actions, and, ultimately, one's feelings."[64]

Coming out of our hiding spots enables us to experience the reality and truth of the gospel and Jesus' redemptive power on a deeper personal level.

This exercise relates to shepherding because caring like a shepherd involves recognizing when sheep have broken legs or wounded hearts, having compassion on them—not adding to shame that's already there—and helping guide others towards healing and wholeness. This exercise can be somewhat uncomfortable, yet the potential of freedom in your soul will outweigh the potential anxiety of sharing. You can do it! Your freedom is worth the risk. Let's experience God's compassion for one another.

SUGGESTED TIME: 90 minutes
SUPPLIES: Blank sheet of paper; something to write with
GROUP SETUP: In a circle; a private place free of distractions
GROUP LEADER PREPARATION: None

OBJECTIVES:

- To understand the nature of shame, conviction, and condemnation
- To identify an event in your life that caused shame and share it with safe people
- To receive a measure of healing, release, and freedom on an individual level
- To continue to go deeper in community, connecting at the soul level

DIRECTIONS:

Warm-Up Stage (15 minutes):

1. Pray together, thanking God that he is the Father of compassion, that he is safe, that he loves to redeem and heal the soul, and that his gospel has the power to give freedom and deep peace.

2. Now talk about the following questions as a group:

---

64   Ibid., 83.

- For this exercise it's important to be a safe person. How does the character of God show us that he is a safe place to bring our deepest secrets?
- How can we reflect his character in regard to being a safe place for others so that they can be vulnerable around us?

Working Stage (60 minutes):

Take time to think and pray on your own on "Gauge" and "Reshape" (see below), then move on to the group steps of "Share" and "Speak out."

3. **Gauge**: On a scale of 1–10, gauge how closely you identify with this statement: "If people find out who I really am, they wouldn't like me." (1 being I don't identify with the statement at all; 10 being I completely identify with it).

4. **Reshape**: "Thus, the key to overcoming shame is more than simply learning to love and accept oneself; it is to discern God's perspective on one's shame and guilt, and to let his perspective drive and reshape one's thoughts, actions, and, ultimately, one's feelings."[65] Use the table on p. 178 with the following headings to let God's perspective reshape any shameful beliefs. One of the lines has been filled in as an example.

---

65   Ibid., 83.

(1) Shameful core belief about myself	(2) Behavior caused by belief	(3) Resulting feeling	(4) What would Jesus say?	(5) Balanced statement
I am worthless.	I don't set healthy boundaries.	Lonely Weak Insecure	You are worth so much to me that I died for you.	People, including myself, may have treated me as worthless in the past, but Jesus declares me worthy, so I can now live accordingly.

5. **Share**: Split up into gender specific groups and share your table with those in the group.

6. **Speak out**: Have one person in the group read God's truths from the table columns (4) and (5) out loud over you.

Cool Down Stage (15 minutes):

7. Go around and share what your comfort level is right now on a scale of 1–10? (1 being very comfortable; 10 being extremely uncomfortable). Acknowledge that it is normal to feel somewhat exposed after sharing such personal information. Use this moment to show each other that everyone is still accepted and loved, even after they have shared. Some people may experience this reaction of unconditional love and acceptance for the first time in their life.

8. Pray for each other in pairs.

> **Shepherding individuals** are uniquely gifted by Jesus to care for the soul and create connections, inspiring **community and healing**.

8

The Teaching Exercises
Exegeting, Explaining, Enlightening

The teacher loves to dig deep into information and knowledge and then teach it to others. The disciples recognized this gift in Jesus' life: "You call me Teacher and Lord, and you are right, for so I am" (John 13:13). The Pharisees also acknowledged his powerful ability, "Rabbi, we know that you are a teacher come from God, for no one can do these signs that you do unless God is with him" (John 3:2). Even the general public distinguished his teaching from the normal teachers of the day, "And they were astonished at his teaching, for he taught them as one who had authority, and not as the scribes" (Mark 1:22). Jesus then distributed this gift to some to be equippers in the church (Ephesians 4:7–8, 11). Teachers (Greek *didaskalos*) have the authority and ability given by God to bring light to the Scripture, exegeting it, and explaining it to the body.

When a church has a healthy teaching culture, people know the Word of God. There is a hunger for the Word, and there is an atmosphere of learning, wisdom, understanding, and application. As should be the case with all five, there will be pathways available to equip more teachers.

God's Word is a treasure, and good teachers are invaluable to the body of Christ. They excite others as they reveal the riches of the Bible. They also protect the body from unsound doctrine, and they often write and develop curriculum. On one end of the spectrum of maturity, as believers we are all encouraged in Colossians 3:16 to, "Let the word of Christ dwell in you richly, teaching and admonishing one another in all wisdom," and on the other end, some teachers will mature to the point of equipping others to become teachers.

Teachers typically have an insatiable appetite for knowledge and learning. There is a danger they can get absorbed in endless learning; thus, their gift can be complemented well by an apostle who will come in and exclaim, "Alright, enough studying, let's do something about it!" (i.e., let's not just acquire information—let's apply it).

Equally vital as the other four gifts for the Great Commission, the teacher's role is to make disciples in the aspect of teaching others to obey everything Jesus had commanded (see Matthew 28:20). In a Western world that tends to be "over-educated yet under-obedient,"[66] the following equipping activities will focus on obedience in the form of application, motivated by love for Christ. "If you love me, you will keep my commands," Jesus says in John 14:15. James expresses it this way: "But don't just listen to God's word. You must do what it says. Otherwise, you are only fooling yourselves" (James 1:22, NLT).

> **Teaching individuals** are uniquely gifted by Jesus to give instruction in the Word of God, inspiring **clear understanding and application**.

The following exercises will help everyone grow in awareness and application of teaching.

Preview of teaching equipping exercises:

> **Equipping Exercise 1**: How to Study the Bible to Teach to Others
> **Equipping Exercise 2**: Potpourri Topical Bible Study
> **Equipping Exercise 3**: Crafting Creative and Compelling Questions
> **Equipping Exercise 4**: Meditating on the Word of God
> **Equipping Exercise 5**: Facilitating a Dynamic Bible Study

---

66 Neil Cole, *Organic Leadership: Leading Naturally Right Where You Are*, (Michigan: Baker Books, 2010), 208.

Teaching Equipping Exercises

Equipping Exercise 1: How To Study The Bible To Teach To Others

This foundational teaching exercise will help you learn how to systematically read, study, and teach a passage of Scripture. This method is called an inductive Bible study. Broadly speaking, it involves a process of dissecting the passage by making observations, interpreting it by deciphering what it means, and applying it to your life by taking action.[67]

SUGGESTED TIME: 90 minutes
SUPPLIES: Bible and copies of this exercise template and something to write with
GROUP SETUP: None
GROUP LEADER PREPARATION: None

OBJECTIVES:

• To gain a basic working knowledge of how to prepare any passage of the Bible to teach
• To grow in the area of expositional teaching
• To be able to deconstruct a passage in the Bible, then reconstruct it so as to teach to others

DIRECTIONS:

Warm-Up Stage (5 minutes):

1. Begin by asking Jesus, our Teacher, to illuminate the Scripture through the Holy Spirit.

Working Stages (20 minutes each):

2. **Dissect with Observations** (20 minutes):

---

67 The framework for this exercise was adapted from Howard G. Hendricks and William D. Hendricks, *Living by the Book: The Art and Science of Reading the Bible*, (Illinois: Moody Publishers, 2007).

Begin to make observations of the passage by going through the following questions. You can choose any Bible passage, but often it's helpful to look at a section of Scripture your church is currently focusing on. Alternatively, you could look at the Ephesians 4:1–16 passage we have examined throughout this book. Write your thoughts in the spaces below:

Who is writing or speaking and to whom?

What is the passage about in general?

Where does this take place?

When does this take place?

Why does the speaker or author say/write what he does—what is his motivation?

Are there commands to obey?

Are there promises that can be claimed in Jesus' name?

Are there positive examples to follow?

Are there errors to learn from?

Are there sins to avoid?

What are the cause/effect relationships?

What are the repeated words and ideas?

What are the significant connecting words that help you understand the author's argument (e.g., *therefore, but, and,* etc.)?

What problems were the recipients facing?

Are there any contrasts or comparisons?

Is there a main word of the passage that would be beneficial to look up in Hebrew/Greek to add value to the study?

In reading different translations (YLT, NASB, ESV, NLT, MSG) what jumps out?

What do I learn about God the Father?

What do I learn about Jesus?

What do I learn about the Holy Spirit?

What do I learn about people in general?

What do I learn about myself?

3. **Decipher the Interpretation** (20 minutes):

Now that many observations have been made and you have broken down the passage into nuts and bolts, we are going to reconstruct it and look at the big picture. This involves zooming out to decipher the original meaning of the passage as a whole. To aid with this, here are a few questions to filter through. Write your responses in the space provided:

What does the passage mean in light of the whole chapter?

What does the passage mean in light of the whole book?

What's the original meaning in the culture of the day? (A commentary may be helpful.)

Do commentaries bring clarity to any difficult verse/s?

Are there any cross-references that would bring light to the meaning of the passage?

Using the repeated words, ideas, and commands I observed, how would I summarize the passage in one sentence?

4. **Do It—the Application** (20 minutes):

As humans, we are naturally curious and desire to gain more knowledge, but we cannot stop there. God gave us his Word to transform our lives; therefore, the culmination of the inductive Bible study needs to be applying the passage to our lives—*doing* what the Word says. If we frame it in the Great Commission, this means teaching *to obey* everything Jesus has commanded us. While there are clear boundaries God intended for interpreting the meaning of Scripture, there are various applications, as each person is unique. Think about the questions below to help stimulate application and write your responses in the space provided:

How can I live this out in everyday life?

Is there a general command to obey for my life?

Is there a promise I can claim in Jesus' name?

Is there a positive example to follow?

Is there an error I can learn from?

Is there something that convicted me of sin that I need to confess or avoid?

What thought pattern will I change as a result of this passage?

What habit can I develop based on this passage?

Who do I know who might also be interested in this theme/topic/principle? When will I pass on to them what I've learned?

It's very easy to be enthusiastic about doing something, but then forget about it, or try hard to implement it in your life and then fail. Remember to ask the Holy Spirit to be the engine that empowers this application. "For God is working in you, giving you the desire and the power to do what pleases him" Philippians 2:13 (NLT).

When you teach the Word, it's always good to close with a prayer of dependence on him and trust in his power.

Cool Down Stage (25 minutes):

5. **Create an Outline**

Using the outline on page 204, create a framework for your teaching, with three main blocks that parallel the exercises above. You don't have to include every answer from the questions above. In order to avoid information overload or becoming mechanical, make sure you ask the Holy Spirit what should be included from your notes and what is not relevant for this time.

I. Observations, adding the verse references in order of the verses studied

II. Interpretation

III. Applications

Later, in Equipping Exercise 3, you will be creating compelling questions that will help enrich your content, so that those you are teaching engage with the text and consider its meaning for their own lives.

Teaching Equipping Exercises

Equipping Exercise 2: Potpourri Topical Bible Study

Teaching verse by verse through a passage of the Bible has great advantages, yet it can also be fascinating and fun to study specific topics, such as anger, abortion, money, Messianic prophecy, parenting, or to look at a particular biblical character, such as Paul. This exercise will equip you to prepare and teach a topical Bible study to a group.

SUGGESTED TIME: 60 minutes or so depending on the number of groups
SUPPLIES: Bibles (including glossary and a Bible concordance), notebooks, and something to write with
GROUP SETUP: Groups of 3 or 4
GROUP LEADER PREPARATION: None

OBJECTIVES:

- To gain wisdom and understanding on difficult topics in the Bible
- To work together and, as a body of Christ, add the riches of revelation together to present a clear teaching on the topic

DIRECTIONS:

Warm-Up Stage (5 minutes):

1. Pray, asking the Holy Spirit to illuminate the Scriptures and enlighten the eyes of our hearts for understanding on these potentially difficult or controversial topics.

2. Ask each person to write down a topic on a small piece of paper and throw the paper into a bowl.

3. Ask each group of three or four to draw out one topic.

Working Stage Part I (30 minutes):

4. **Study** the topic in the Scriptures using the glossary in the back of a study Bible, a topical concordance, or a Bible App to dig up verses relevant to the topic. You can make notes in the space below, using this suggested structure:

What do the verses say about this topic in relation to God/Jesus/Holy Spirit?

What do the verses say about this topic in relation to people in general (us)?

What's the crucial point of the matter? e.g., what is God's perspective?

Keeping in mind the goal of discipleship, where the key is *teaching to obey* what the Lord has commanded us, how will you apply the Bible's wisdom on the chosen topic to your lives?

Working Stage Part II (20 minutes):

5. **Present** your topic to the other groups.

6. **Pass it on**: The groups that were listening to the presented topic now gather back in their group and summarize what they heard presented from the other group. This will help with retention and being "prepared to give an answer to everyone who asks you to give the reason for the hope that you have" (1 Peter 3:15 NIV) to both believers and non-believers. You can jot some notes here:

7. **Rotate** until all groups have taught their topics and subsequently allowed time for the recipients to gather in their own groups and summarize the key message they heard.

Cool Down Stage (5 minutes):

8. Reflect individually on the following two questions, writing your thoughts below:

What are you taking away from this teaching exercise in general?

Do you feel like you grew according to the exercise objectives? How?

9. Close in prayer.

Teaching Equipping Exercises

Equipping Exercise 3: Crafting Creative and Compelling Questions

Crafting creative and compelling questions is essential in teaching, as the goal is not only to exegete the text, but to help those you are teaching to engage with the text and think for themselves. Remember, we want to make *mature* disciples, as Ephesians 4:13 says, and part of that means fostering the ability of believers to think for themselves. This is accomplished by asking powerful, thought-provoking questions. This exercise will enable you to formulate questions that will do just that, and by doing so, move participants from passive recipients to active contributors.[68]

SUGGESTED TIME: 50 minutes
SUPPLIES: A Bible, something to write with, and paper
GROUP SETUP: None
GROUP LEADER PREPARATION: None

OBJECTIVE:

- To learn how to craft engaging questions as part of teaching the Bible

DIRECTIONS:

Warm-Up Stage (5 minutes):

1. **Begin with prayer**, thanking Jesus for his example of asking compelling questions as a teacher. Ask him to continue to mature us as teachers, in his likeness, and to grant creativity in generating questions.

2. **Select** a small portion of Scripture you want to focus on. Crafting questions will mirror the three levels of How to Study the Bible to Teach to Others in Teaching Equipping Exercise 1.

---

68   The general concept of this exercise was based on Joyce MacKichan Walker, "The Art of Asking Good Questions: the Role of Questions in Discussion," available to download at www.thethoughtfulchristian.com .

Working Stage (35 minutes):

3. **Craft five "Dissecting" questions** from the text that can be answered by simple observation. These are primarily "Who, What, Where, When, Why" questions, and are used to highlight important facts and details. If you get stuck, great examples of these can be found in the "Dissect it" section in Teaching Equipping Exercise 1. For example, if you were looking at the Ephesians 4:11–16 text, a couple of specific *dissecting* questions you might ask would be:

   - *What* are the five gifts that Jesus gave to the church?
   - From verse 12, *why* does it say he gave these gifts?

Write your five *dissecting* questions here:

4. **Craft three "Deciphering" questions**: These questions will mirror the "Decipher the Interpretation" section of Teaching Equipping Exercise 1 and help others interpret and understand the meaning of the passage. In contrast to the previous set of questions, these questions take longer to formulate and more time to answer. Additionally, they will have a range of possible answers. Continuing with our specific passage of Ephesians, a few examples of *deciphering* questions could be:

   - What characterizes each of these five gifts?
   - How were each of those five used in the early church, and how are they used today?
   - What does it look like practically to equip the saints for the work of ministry?

Write your three *deciphering* questions here:

5. **Craft three "Doing" questions**: These will move participants to personalize the text and action it in their life. The application will vary for each person as there are no right or wrong answers (unless, of course, a response goes against God's character, his Word, or is spiritually harmful for the person or someone else, e.g., "I want to read my Bible more so that God will love me more").

    Examples of *doing* questions in line with our text could be:

    - In an area of the fivefold where you are stronger, what one practical step could you take to equip someone else in this area?
    - In an area of the fivefold where you are weaker, what one practical step could you take to be equipped by someone else in this area?

Write your three *doing* questions here:

Cool Down Stage (10 minutes):

6. **Get feedback**: Exchange your written questions with someone who can give you honest feedback. They should be looking for whether the questions fit the category, whether the questions are creative and compelling, and whether they elicit a helpful response. Note their feedback here as a reference for the future crafting of creative and compelling questions:

Teaching Equipping Exercises

Equipping Exercise 4: Meditating on the Word of God

In today's noisy world, life is rushed and hectic, and even our time in the Bible can become rushed, preventing us from truly ingesting and digesting Scripture. This exercise challenges us to slow down, meditate on God's Word, and let it sink in. It follows the schematic of *lectio divina* (Latin for "divine reading"), yet another way to learn how to engage with Scripture. *Lectio divina* has been likened to "feasting on the Word":

- first, the taking of a bite (*lectio*);
- then chewing on it (*meditatio*);
- savoring its essence (*oratio*); and
- digesting it and making it a part of the body (*contemplatio*).[69]

Rather than treating Scripture as a text to be studied, *lectio divina* views it as the living Word.[70] In contrast to eastern meditation practices of emptying your mind and soul (which are not endorsed), this exercise focuses on filling your mind and soul with the very words of God. Simply stated, it follows a progression of reading the Word, thinking deeply about the significance of it, responding in prayer, and finally, resting in silence as it's contemplated.

SUGGESTED TIME: 40 minutes
SUPPLIES: A Bible and something to write with
GROUP SETUP: A quiet place without interruption
GROUP LEADER PREPARATION: Selecting a portion of Scripture in advance that is not too long. Some suggested passages are Psalm 23, Psalm 131, John 10:10–18, or John 15:1–13

---

69   Gervase Holdaway, *The Oblate Life* (Minnesota: Liturgical Press, 2008), 109.
70   David G. Benner, *Opening to God: Lectio Divina and Life as Prayer* (Illinois: IVP Books, 2010), 47–53.

OBJECTIVES:

- To promote communion with God
- To grow in the knowledge of his Word
- To recognize the benefits of slowing down and resting in God's presence and peace

DIRECTIONS:

Warm-Up Stage (5 minutes):

1. After finding a quiet place to do this exercise, take time to pray to invite God's presence, to calm your heart and mind, and to lead you in this time. If disruptive thoughts come to mind, jot them down on a notepad to the side. If needed, put on soft piano music in the background. Repeat Psalm 46:10 to yourself, "Be still, and know that I am God."

Working Stage (30 minutes or more, do not rush):

2. **Read the Word:** Taking the portion of Scripture selected, choose two different people to read it aloud slowly and allow it to speak to your hearts. During this time, those not reading are allowing the words spoken to flow over them and asking God, "Which word or phrase do you want me to hear?" In his book *The Practice of Godliness*, Jerry Bridges explains:

> The Holy Spirit leads us *objectively* through the general teaching of His word. This is where we learn His will for all Christians. But the Holy Spirit also leads us *subjectively* as He impresses certain Scriptures on our minds, applying them to specific situations in our lives. This is His way of showing us what He wants us to give attention to at a particular time, this is the way He leads us to establish a priority of applications.[71]

---

71 Jerry Bridges, *The Practice of Godliness* (Colorado: NavPress, 1996), 65.

Write down the word or phrase that the Holy Spirit is impressing on your heart:

3. **Reflect in meditation**: Next we reflect on what has been read by thinking deeply with God: *Which word or phrase was impressed upon my heart? Where does this touch my life?* 1 Corinthians 2:10 tells us "these things God has revealed to us through the Spirit. For the Spirit searches everything, even the depths of God." Take five minutes to reflect in silent meditation. Each person is then invited to share their reflections with others.

Write your own reflections here:

Write others' reflections here:

4. **Respond in prayer**: Read the portion of Scripture slowly aloud a third time. The question of focus here is: Holy Spirit, how should I respond to this word or phrase?

    This is the life application part as we follow the Great Commission in teaching to *obey* everything he has commanded us. Take five minutes to speak to God and dialogue with him, pausing to listen after asking the question. He loves you and delights in hearing from you. For some, journaling these thoughts of prayer may help. Once that time has passed, feel free to share with others how you sense the Lord asking you to respond.

Write your prayer of response here:

5. **Rest in contemplation**: Whether it's climbing into bed after a long day and falling asleep, or taking a break from studying, it always feels good to rest. Contemplate this experience as you rest in silence for a few final minutes. When our soul needs rest, Jesus exhorts us, "Come to me, all who labor and are heavy laden, and I will give you rest" (Matthew 11:28). As you rest, fear may try to creep in as you think about what it looks like to implement your response to the text, but keep your mind focused on Jesus and his perfect love, which drives out all fear (see 1 John 4:18).

Cool Down Stage (5 minutes):

6. How do you feel about *lectio divina* as an approach to teaching Scripture? Briefly share answers with each other.

7. Ask one another if you are happy to hold each other accountable to the things you want to respond to (from Step 4).

8. Discuss any common themes that were shared during this time. Sometimes the Spirit is trying to communicate something to the entire group or church.

Teaching Equipping Exercises

Equipping Exercise 5: Facilitating a Dynamic Bible Study

There are many components to teaching and delivering a dynamic Bible study. In the previous teaching exercises, the focus has been mainly on content development. Delivering that content is the focus of this exercise, and doing it in such a way that facilitates conversation and spiritual growth. Moderation may not come naturally, and therefore it is a valuable skill to be learned and cultivated. Moderation is about asking the right questions, giving others a voice, listening, empowering people to discover, guiding people deeper, and summarizing.

SUGGESTED TIME: 45 minutes
SUPPLIES: Bibles, something to write with
GROUP SETUP: Chairs in a circle
GROUP LEADER PREPARATION: Be ready to facilitate the content for this exercise

OBJECTIVE:

• To develop the skill of facilitation as part of teaching

DIRECTIONS:

Warm-Up Stage (5 minutes):

1. Begin with prayer, asking the Lord to bless the time and to be guided by the flow of his Spirit.

2. From Exercise 1 or elsewhere, use content from a passage of the Bible you are studying together.

3. From Exercise 3 or elsewhere, use questions you have formulated.

4. Shortly review whatever your content or main point was from the previous week—people are forgetful and new people may be present.

Working Stage (30 minutes):

5. As you present the content of the Bible, focus on implementing these facilitation principles:

    *   **"See" each person**: calling on people specifically to read text and to answer questions makes them feel seen and involved.

    *   **Ask questions**: asking lots of questions keeps people engaged.

    *   **Allow silence**: it's your friend. With questions, it allows time for people to think, and between parts, silence allows people to digest.

    *   **Don't degrade**: refrain from shooting someone down if they respond unusually—ask them "How do you know that to be true?" Or defer to the group by inquiring, "What do you all think?"—always compare responses to what the Bible says.

    *   **Give everyone a voice**: to do so, you'll need to regulate introverts and extroverts. The extroverts often need to be toned down; the introverts usually need to be activated to ensure their voice is heard.

    *   **Balance structure and flow**: be prepared to lay down the plan of getting through all the Bible study to go with the flow of the Holy Spirit. One question may stimulate the group to deeper things, which are more important in that moment than finishing everything you wanted to get through.

Cool Down Stage (10 minutes):

6. **Summarize**: based on what has been shared over the past half hour. As the facilitator, verbally summarize the group's input, overarching theme, and any final principle from you.

7. **Feedback**: allow each member to give the facilitator feedback. What did they do well? What's an area they could work on? Jot some notes of people's feedback here:

8. **Close in prayer**

> **Teaching individuals** are uniquely gifted by Jesus to give instruction in the Word of God, inspiring **clear understanding and application**.

Final Thoughts:
Synergy for the Kingdom

Remember the orchestra analogy at the beginning of this book? Now when the violinist hands you the instrument to play, instead of shock, you can smile, taking it in your hands, knowing how to smoothly and confidently make beautiful music with the rest of the orchestra. *You have been equipped.* And as Beau Crosetto reminds us, "God gives us gifts to play a beautiful symphony, not a solo."[72] I hope you have enjoyed engaging with the variety of equipping exercises throughout this training manual. I hope you have grown stronger in your faith, in your understanding of the five gifts of Jesus, and discovered where your strengths lie, so you can equip others in that area and glorify Jesus.

Jesus Christ, in all of his fullness and glory, is our supreme apostle, the most powerful prophet, the divine embodiment of the evangelistic good news, the chief shepherd, and the teacher with unrivalled authority. Since Christ is our ultimate role model, we should desire to emulate him in all five of these aspects, both on an individual and a church body level. We should allow his pulse to pump through our spiritual veins. Ephesians is clear "we are to grow up in every way into him who is the head, into Christ" (4:15). As modelled by Jesus with his followers, true discipleship growth will involve practical application: learning by doing, not simply information that puffs up our knowledge.

Here are the questions I want to pose as we conclude: have you as an individual developed into the fullness of Christ? Has your church reached unity in the faith, in the knowledge of the Son of God and matured to the fullness of Christ? Since the answer to these rhetorical questions has to be no, as none of us will attain full maturity this side of heaven, we need to passionately pursue the fivefold ministry until Jesus returns.

---

72 Beau Crosetto et al., *Release the APE: An Onramp to Activating Apostolic, Prophetic and Evangelistic Leaders* (Exponential Resources, 2014), Kindle edition.

If we deny the reality of our status quo, the results will be drastic. If an apostolic environment is not cultivated, the mission of God will suffer. The kingdom will not expand to its potential, since new ministries and churches will not be pioneered. The people of God will not progress forward, disciple-making movements will not be present, and a healthy foundation for the other four areas will be absent. Without prophetic insight, we will not have guidance, vision, clarity, or direction. There will be a lack of strengthening, encouragement, and comforting for the body. God's presence and his holiness won't be honored among believers, and his passion for righteousness and social justice won't be displayed in the world. The status quo will reign, and the call for change will not be issued. Continuing onward, if evangelistic equipping doesn't happen, there will be a shortage of outward focus. Lost people, unreconciled to their heavenly Father, will continue living and dying without hope. The good news of the gospel will not go forth, and there will be no saved people to shepherd, teach, encourage, or send out to reach their own circle. Furthermore, without shepherds, who care for individuals on a heart and soul level, there will be no mutual care amongst the body, and there will be a cold, impersonal atmosphere. People will not feel safe to open up and to be vulnerable, hindering inner healing. The dynamic of community won't develop, so gatherings will feel more like an academic course or worldly event, rather than the warm, accepting spiritual family of God. And lastly, if potential teachers are not equipped or, in general, a teaching environment isn't cultivated, the body will not mature. Scriptures will neither be enlightened nor explained, and our roots will be shallow. Sound doctrine will give way to contemporary trends, compromising the Word of God.

Indeed, we are desperate for the fullness of Christ—desperate to expand beyond the present twofold expression of shepherd and teacher and into the full fivefold expression. Not only for the relief of overburdened pastors, but more so for the greater purpose of a healthier, multidimensional, more powerful display of Jesus' glory in this world. The fivefold ministry isn't a model of doing church, or one option to choose from; it is the biblical blueprint Jesus gave us for how the church should function to display his fullness. We need to pursue all five.

PEOPLE, PATHWAYS, AND PRACTICES

To pursue and see all five pumping through the body, I want to leave you with a simple three-word strategy to keep in mind: *People, Pathways,* and *Practices.*

First, identify five *people* who healthily and maturely model one particular dimension of Jesus' ministry. Remember, the five functions are like seeds latent in the system. There are already individuals in your church, team, or organization who have a measure of each gift. By talking with others about their core passions and concerns, and through the practical exercises in this training manual, it will become very clear which individuals are the most healthy and mature in each area. *Do you know who healthily models each dimension of fivefold ministry?*

Second, create clear *pathways* of equipping to help grow in awareness and application towards maturity. Everyone has a measure of grace in each area, but may be very early on the journey, or may not see the path to walk on. Ideally, those who have been identified as mature in one particular gift should lead others down the respective pathways. Essentially these exercises provide equipping pathways to walk people through. Of course, the path can continue beyond these exercises, and the pathways can and should be extended for those who have demonstrated gifting and hunger to grow more. *Do you have clear pathways in place for people to walk down?*

Third, weave *practices* into your organizational culture that include *language* and *license*.[73] Fivefold ministry needs to be woven into the culture you're part of if you want it to stick and have long-lasting impact. Think about developing a common *language* for the fivefold as a team or leadership, talking about it regularly, and casting vision for it. For example, for the prophetic, this might look like:

- agreeing what it means to be prophetic, such as using language of "helping people pursue God in prayer and worship," "speaking out God's heart for encouragement," and "challenging the status quo";
- talking about the prophetic regularly so that you communicate it's something you value; and
- casting vision for being a community that pursues God's heart and rights the wrongs in this world.

License involves giving people permission to create their respective fivefold environment in the church, and empowering them to do things they're called to do. Think about motivating, empowering, releasing, and sending those within your organization. Identify, celebrate, and release the apostles, for example, within the church. Give them permission to pioneer new things in the neighborhood. Have you incorporated steps for *language* and *license* for each of the five dimensions?

---

73   Quoted from Brad Brisco in "APEST A" in https://vimeo.com/287156868 , (accessed May 23, 2019).

SYNERGY FOR THE KINGDOM

In the opening chapters of this book, I attempted to lay out a clear and concise biblical case for recognizing, equipping, and releasing the five ministry areas in Ephesians 4. It is upon that foundation that the exercises you have now completed are built upon—exercises that will both activate and cultivate this blueprint in our individual lives, as well as our gathered, communal times together as the church.

I truly believe if we do this, we will see a healthier, more powerful, and fully unified display of Jesus. Disciples of Jesus will be trained and multiplied, and God's mission of filling the earth with his glory will come to pass. As these five ministry areas integrate, the synergy they create will generate a vortex of power that will transform this world around us.

No longer operating as individual ministry circles, the fivefold spheres are interacting, converging, working together as a body should. Remember, Ephesians 4:16 emphasizes the joints—"the whole body, joined and held together by every joint with which it is equipped"—which guides us beyond the individual's gift discovery into the intersection, the relational connections, the gift integration and synergy between people in the body of Christ.

This integration will be challenging, however, due to opposition from our flesh and the enemy. Since each area has a different purpose and different perspective, the core concerns will pull in different directions. Missiologist and church planter JR Woodward notes a specific example of this tension, when

> people gifted in one area tend to judge others not similarly gifted. For example, the budding evangelist would criticize those in the group who didn't have a similar heart for those outside of the kingdom. What budding evangelists need to know is that God wants to use them to bring that heart to the rest of the group.[74]

So beware, the enemy will strive to create division amongst these ministries and amongst people. If this truly is Jesus' blueprint for the church—the most powerful change agent in the world—it makes sense that the enemy will fight against the development of the five equipping areas. He wants to make the church body limp, lethargic, disconnected and, as a result, ineffective. We can counter this spiritual warfare in prayer and in behavior by honoring and appreciating the differences of others, as "in humility [we] count others more significant than [our]selves" (Philippians 2:3). As we noted in chapter two, humility is the onramp for unity. And unity is essential for synergy.

---

74   Woodward, *Creating a Missional Culture*, 204.

When each part of the body is equipped—that is, put in the right position to function—and exercised, it will grow. And grow … and grow … and grow … "until we all attain to the unity of the faith and of the knowledge of the Son of God, to mature manhood, to the measure of the stature of the fullness of Christ" (Ephesians 4:13). What a beautiful picture. What a beautiful vision.

Clearly, all believers can grow and develop in the apostolic, prophetic, evangelistic, shepherding, and teaching to become more like Christ in character and ministry. In each of us, it is simply his grace that pumps through our body, as well as the body worldwide, providing impulses to accomplish this. In *Primal Fire*, Neil Cole leaves us with an inspiring vision:

> Imagine a kingdom ruled by Jesus, where each person has direct contact with the King and moves at His impulse. Imagine what our loving and all-knowing Creator could do with a body so responsive to His voice.[75]

Do you long to see the whole body activated? Responsive to his voice? A synergy for the kingdom that is beyond anything we have experienced thus far in history?

Then pass on this training manual.

Gather a few others together and equip them!

I'm praying that God does a work in us, and through us, to spread his kingdom.

Let your kingdom come, Jesus.
Come, Lord Jesus, come.

---

75   Cole with Kaak, Helfer, Baker and Waken, *Primal Fire*, 37.

Bonus Material

His Pulse In You—The Gospel of the Kingdom

You may see church buildings around you in your city, and you may have even grown up with Christian religious lessons in your school, but have you ever really made a decision to allow him to be part of you? Literally, indwell you? You see, to have him pump spiritual energy and life through your veins, *you need his Spirit inside of you*. Makes sense, right? God says, "I will give you a new heart, and a new spirit I will put within you. And I will remove the heart of stone from your flesh and give you a heart of flesh" (Ezekiel 36:26).[76] He wants to give you a new heart, a new life! God's Word tells us, "Therefore, if anyone is in Christ, he is a new creation. The old has passed away; behold, the new has come" (2 Corinthians 5:17).

How do you get this new life? How do you get the source of life, Jesus, living inside of you? A high-ranking Jewish teacher in Israel asked Jesus that very same question. We pick up the conversation in the book of John:

"Rabbi, we know that you are a teacher come from God, for no one can do these signs that you do unless God is with him." Jesus answered him, "Truly, truly, I say to you, unless one is born again he cannot see the kingdom of God." Nicodemus said to him, "How can a man be born when he is old? Can he enter a second time into his mother's womb and be born?" Jesus answered, "Truly, truly, I say to you, unless one is born of water and the Spirit, he cannot enter the kingdom of God. That which is born of the flesh is flesh, and that which is born of the Spirit is spirit. Do not marvel that I said to you, 'You must be born again.'"

John 3: 2-7

---

76   Originally this verse was spoken to the nation of Israel, to redeem a people for himself to show his power and his glory, yet God's heart is still the same and can be applied to us individually today. For example, God tells us in the New Testament in 1 Peter 2:9, "But you are a chosen race, a royal priesthood, a holy nation, a people for his own possession, that you may proclaim the excellencies of him who called you out of darkness into his marvelous light."

To be born again, Jesus talks about seeing and entering the kingdom of God. Entering the kingdom of God hints that being born again is about something greater, something much bigger than just you—a whole kingdom—so let's unpack this before coming back to you personally.

I'm not sure what your first association with the word "kingdom" is, but when I think of a "kingdom," I think of a *king*—someone who reigns fairly, with love, justice, and righteousness. This may be hard to imagine, because, like all of us, rulers and politicians are sinful and therefore do not reign with love, justice, and righteousness. This only underscores the reality that this whole world is broken and requires restoration. We need a new system and a new king! Enter Jesus Christ. Now Christ isn't a last name, but rather a title. Christ actually means "anointed one, God's chosen King."[77] Throughout the whole Bible, his arrival had been predicted, and the theme of this coming King and his coming kingdom is central. The Bible is one overarching story about God's love and his mission to redeem this world through his Son. Here are just a few examples in the Old Testament where this King and kingdom is foretold:

- Daniel wrote regarding the King of Persia, nearly 550 years before Jesus was born, "Then King Darius wrote to all the peoples, nations, and languages that dwell in all the earth: 'Peace be multiplied to you. I make a decree, that in all my royal dominion people are to tremble and fear before the God of Daniel, for he is the living God, enduring forever; his kingdom shall never be destroyed, and his dominion shall be to the end. He delivers and rescues; he works signs and wonders in heaven and on earth, he who has saved Daniel from the power of the lions'" (Daniel 6:25–26).

- Zechariah 9:9 foreshadows Palm Sunday, before Good Friday and Easter, when Jesus would ride into the city of Jerusalem and be celebrated as a coming King: "Behold, your king is coming to you; righteous and having salvation is he, humble and mounted on a donkey..."

- Another prophecy, approximately 700 years before Jesus came, citing the character of the coming King and his government, is found in Isaiah 9:6–7, "For to us a child is born, to us a son is given; and the government shall be upon his shoulder, and his name shall be called Wonderful Counselor, Mighty God, Everlasting Father, Prince of Peace. Of the increase of his government and of peace there will be no end, on the throne of David and over his kingdom, to establish it and to uphold it with justice and with righteousness from this time forth and forevermore."

---

77 Vine's Expository Dictionary, *Christos*, Blue Letter Bible, https://www.blueletterbible.org/lang/lexicon/lexicon.cfm?strongs=G5547 (accessed September 24, 2019).

- Historians document the scroll (book) written by Micah to approximately 700 years before Christ is born, where he correctly foretells the birthplace of the King, "O Bethlehem [...] from you shall come forth for me one who is to be ruler in Israel" (Micah 5:2).

The whole Old Testament is one big fat arrow pointing towards Jesus the King. From the very beginning in Genesis, promises of God's presence, God's King, God's land and God's people make up what the Bible calls "covenants," and they are all woven together to reveal his story of love and mission to redeem the world. The Old Testament story ends with a cliff-hanger, with the people waiting for this supposed coming King, and waiting, and waiting … 400 years of silence.

And then, it happens. The King arrives! He comes not as a triumphant warrior King but as an innocent child, and the events surrounding his birth are recorded in Matthew's Gospel. Several Wise Men travel hundreds of miles and inquire, "Where is he who has been born king of the Jews? For we saw his star when it rose and have come to worship him" (Matthew 2:2).

Under the oppression of Caesar and the Roman Empire, the people began proclaiming this good news that a new King had been born! It was a proclamation that a new King had been crowned and was beginning a new kingdom. The literal meaning of "the gospel" is "good news," and this new King and his kingdom was good news to the people of the day—bringing freedom from oppression and starting a new era of peace and true justice.

When he was thirty years old, Jesus began proactively introducing his kingdom by spreading peace and justice, and challenging people to follow him in this kingdom way of living. One of his followers, Mark, documents an eyewitness account that, "Jesus came into Galilee, proclaiming the gospel of God, and saying, 'The time is fulfilled, and the kingdom of God is at hand; repent and believe in the gospel'" (Mark 1:14–15). Paraphrased, Jesus proclaimed, "It's good news that I'm here; I embody the kingdom—now turn from your old ways, thoughts, and habits (repent), and trust in me (believe)."

Jesus then called people to follow him, inviting them to be with him and get to know him (which speaks of *relationship*), and to imitate him in the things he did (which speaks of a *lifestyle*). Relationship and lifestyle. Not religion.

Jesus powerfully demonstrates his love to others by healing them and setting them free from oppression. At the same time, he condemns the current religious system of the day, continuing to proclaim he's setting up a new kingdom.

Inevitably, this upsets a lot of people, and Jesus is falsely accused at his trial before the Roman governor of Judea:

Pilate said to him, "So you are a king?" Jesus answered, "You say that I am a king. For this purpose I was born and for this purpose I have come into the world—to bear witness to the truth. Everyone who is of the truth listens to my voice." Pilate said to him, "What is truth?" After he had said this, he went back outside to the Jews and told them, "I find no guilt in him. But you have a custom that I should release one man for you at the Passover. So do you want me to release to you the King of the Jews?" They cried out again, "Not this man, but Barabbas!" Now Barabbas was a robber.

John 18:37-40

Pilate said to them, "Then what shall I do with Jesus who is called Christ?" They all said, "Let him be crucified!" And he said, "Why, what evil has he done?" But they shouted all the more, "Let him be crucified!"

Matthew 27:22-23

Innocent Jesus takes the penalty of the true prisoner (Barabbas), and the guilty prisoner, who deserved the penalty, receives freedom. This passage is deeply symbolic, and is still applicable to us today. We are the guilty prisoner, and the freedom offered to Barabbas is offered to us too:

For God made Christ, who never sinned, to be the offering for our sin, so that we could be made right with God through Christ.

2 Corinthians 5:21 NLT

Giving into political pressure, Pilate gives Jesus over to be brutally scourged and crucified, hanging six hours on a cross, in what is potentially the most excruciating way to die. In an unprecedented act of love, Jesus, as King of all, chose to die for his people.

For God so loved the world, that he gave his only Son, that whoever believes in him should not perish but have eternal life. For God did not send his Son into the world to condemn the world, but in order that the world might be saved through him.

John 3:16-17

In the culture of the day, a gospel (remember, "good news") was an announcement that a military battle had been won, and therefore a new king had been crowned and would set up his kingdom. On that cross, Jesus won the spiritual battle against sin and Satan! But the supposed King was now laying in a tomb, dead. And Caesar was still on the throne. At first glance, all hope was lost. Jesus' followers were scared and ran away, fearing persecution. But then something truly miraculous happened: after laying dead for three days inside a tomb, with a massive stone rolled across the entrance, guarded by highly trained Roman soldiers—Jesus did the impossible. He not only defeated the power of sin and Satan, he rose from the dead—defeating death! The King proved to be victorious! "Death is swallowed up in victory … But thanks be to God, who gives us the victory through our Lord Jesus Christ" (1 Corinthians 15: 55, 57).

After he rose from the dead, it's historically documented that many individuals saw Jesus in person over the next forty days, and he even appeared to a group of five hundred people at once. Then Jesus ascended into heaven, and as part of his ascension, this King gave gifts to each one of us. But that's not the end of the story! The King is coming back!

Daniel foreshadows what is still to come:

"I saw in the night visions, and behold, with the clouds of heaven there came one like a son of man, and he came to the Ancient of Days and was presented before him. And to him was given dominion and glory and a kingdom, that all peoples, nations, and languages should serve him; his dominion is an everlasting dominion, which shall not pass away, and his kingdom one that shall not be destroyed."

Daniel 7:13–14

The last two chapters in the Bible, Revelation 21–22 beautifully describe what the fusion of the kingdom of heaven with earth will be like—a real place with real rivers and real nature; an intoxicating air of joy; a redeemed people without suffering or pain; and a real King. Read the two chapters!

During this in-between time, after the King originally came into this world to set his kingdom in motion, and before he brings it to full fruition, the King invites us to be kingdom-agents. He invites us to be born again and join his team to redeem and restore this world.

So here we are, as promised, coming back full circle to you personally. King Jesus invites you into relationship, to know him for real, and to pattern your lifestyle after him. In order to know the King and enter into the kingdom, we need to be spiritually born again:

- to admit and turn away from our sin;
- to believe that he is the King who won the victory and rose from dead; and
- to begin following him, together with others.

You can make the decision now to be born again by telling God those three things in a sincere prayer. Afterwards, it is a process to begin following King Jesus. To do so, he offers *you* his Spirit, "ask, and it will be given to you […] how much more will the heavenly Father give the Holy Spirit to those who ask him!" (Luke 11: 9, 13).

So, go ahead, ask.

His Spirit will come into you, and regenerate you from the inside out.

It's not just a ticket of forgiveness and an entry to heaven. It has implications for life to the fullest here and now. And it means we can join the King in his ways of restoring this broken world. Right where you are in your unique context, in your occupation and your family, you can start participating in the most exciting kingdom redemption story![78]

So, go ahead, ask.

---

78   If you chose to be spiritually born again, making a decision for Jesus to be *your* King and to begin following him together with others, that's fantastic! I can promise you it's the best decision you've ever made. As I noted, it is a process. Similar to training as an athlete, you will want to grow strong, and it helps to have a personal trainer. So talk to someone who knows the King and tell them what you've decided, and/ or write me an email at Nathan@kyriosministries.org and/or check out more information on one of these websites: https://thefour.com/en/ ; https://courses.goingfarther.net/know-jesus/ .

Recommended Fivefold Reading

Neil Cole with Paul Kaak, Phil Helfer, Dezi Baker and Ed Waken. *Primal Fire: Reigniting the Church with the Five Gifts of Jesus* (Carol Stream: Tyndale Momentum, 2014).

Beau Crosetto et al., *Release the APE: An Onramp to Activating Apostolic, Prophetic and Evangelistic Leaders* (Exponential Resources, 2014). This free eBook can be downloaded at https://exponential.org/resource-ebooks/release-the-ape/ .

Alan Hirsch, *5Q: Reactivating the Original Intelligence and Capacity of the Body of Christ* (Atlanta: 100 Movements Publishing, 2017).

Alan Hirsch and Tim Catchim, *The Permanent Revolution: Apostolic Imagination and Practice for the 21st Century Church* (San Francisco: Jossey-Bass, 2012).

Alan Hirsch and Dave Ferguson, *On the Verge: A Journey into the Apostolic Future of the Church* (Grand Rapids: Zondervan, 2011).

Peyton Jones, *Church Zero: Raising 1st Century Churches out of the Ashes of the 21st Century Church* (Colorado Springs: David C. Cook, 2013).

Ben R. Peters, *Folding Five Ministries Into One Powerful Team* (Maitland: Xulon Press, 2011).

Walt Pilcher, *The Five-Fold Effect: Unlocking Power Leadership for Amazing Results in Your Organization* (Bloomington: WestBowPress, 2013).

Daryl L. Smith and Andrew B. Smith, *Discovering Your Missional Potential: An Encounter with Ephesians 4 and How Jesus Lives It* (100 Movements, 2019).

JR Woodward, *Creating a Missional Culture: Equipping the Church for the Sake of the World* (Westmont: IVP Books, 2012).

About the Author

When he was younger, Nathan dreamed of playing professional soccer in Europe and combining that with a desire to share his faith in Christ. When he left his home in the US behind for Vienna, Austria, he planned to be away for one year before returning to become a business executive back in the US. But God had other plans! Twelve years later, Nathan and his family call Vienna home. Since then, Nathan has lived out his faith on the soccer fields, parks, streets, and coffee shops of Vienna, as well as other parts of Europe, Africa, and the US.

In addition to being an author, as an entrepreneur for Christ, Nathan has helped pioneer soccer ministry in Austria, pastored young adults, led mission trips, taught and preached in multiple countries, and founded a team-based ministry, Kyrios Ministries. Based out of Austria, Kyrios Ministries is an international collective of leaders who are passionate Jesus followers, advancing the kingdom of God by organically making disciples. Together with his wife, Insa, he has planted a church, which has a fivefold paradigm of seeing Jesus and being his body.

In 2018, Nathan became a trainer, coach, and consultant with the 5Q Collective, an international training initiative of Alan Hirsch and Rich Robinson, which seeks to equip churches and organizations to more effectively live out and activate the fivefold ministry of Jesus.

Get in
Touch

I would value your feedback and am happy to answer any questions you have or hear stories of how this training manual blessed you. Please feel free to share testimonies as well. Contact me personally by writing to Nathan@kyriosministries.org

This material can be presented in an interactive workshop format. If you are interested in live workshops or online coaching and cohorts, send me an email or check out the websites below.

If you would like to place a bulk order, please contact me at Nathan@kyriosministries.org

For the fullness of Christ,
Nathan

www.fivefoldtraining.com
www.5qcentral.com
www.kyriosministries.org
Facebook.com/FivefoldTraining